Feeling Good About You

The Journey of Discovery That Leads to Self-Esteem

Sandra V. Abell, MS, LPC, ACC

Feeling Good About You
Published by Inside Jobs Coaching Company
Medford, OR 97504

Manufactured in the United States of America

Library of Congress Cataloging-in-Publication Data
Abell, Sandra

Feeling Good About You
Abell, Sandra

ISBN 978-0-9772537-5-3

For Geno
The love of my life

Contents

Acknowledgments

They say it takes a village to create something wonderful, and in the case of this book, I've been fortunate to have the best possible villagers.

My heartfelt thanks to Gene Abell, Karen Fronek, Jamee Rae Pineda, pk Hallinan, and Debbie Kostal for sharing their talent, wisdom and encouragement.

Also, huge thanks to Align Visual Arts & Communication for a fabulous cover design, and Shannon Young for sharing her great ideas and incredible editing skills.

Without you all, this book would never have happened.

Introduction

When you get out of bed in the morning and look in the mirror, what do you say to yourself? Do you smile and say, "Good morning you incredible person, you!" or do you scowl, grumble, and think or say something negative?

Hopefully you smile, because you're amazing!

You're the only one of your kind, and you're perfect in every way. You are the only one who looks the way you look, thinks the way you think and feels the way you feel. Even if you're an identical twin you are still a one-of-a-kind unique and remarkable individual.

Do you know that? Hopefully you know and honor your uniqueness, and love yourself for it.

If this describes how you feel, then you have positive self-esteem. This is a wonderful thing! When you have good self-esteem, you love and value yourself, and this makes your life happy, and makes it easier to deal with challenges.

However, if you don't love and value yourself, your life is probably unhappy and difficult, and everything is a struggle.

This little book is for you, to help you understand the importance of being gentle and nonjudgmental with yourself, and to support you as you learn to value the amazing person you've always been.

Chapter One: Self-Esteem

WHEN I WAS A child my self-esteem was really low. My little sister was cute, smart, easy-going and funny, and everybody loved her. I probably resented the fact that she came along when I was two and "stole" my parents' attention. In response, I decided there must be something wrong with me and that I was un-loveable. I then became angry and inadvertently drove people away.

My parents were loving and fair. However, my perception was that because they spent more time and attention on my sister (as is necessary with small children) I wasn't as important or valuable as she was.

This began 25 years of feeling "less than" others. I perceived that I wasn't as loveable, valuable, capable or competent as everyone else, and this perception became a self-fulfilling prophecy. I didn't know how to make friends, so my grade school years were mostly lonely. High school was slightly better, but I still didn't feel I had much to offer others, so I didn't have many friends.

My early adult years were also painful. But after several experiences in which I was successful, I began to realize that there might be more to me than I'd given myself credit for.

I paid attention to myself, and started to become clear about who I was, separate from my early childhood experiences. I realized that I'm OK, and actually have much to offer. By the time I was in my 30s I also understood that the opinions of others did not define who I was. *Only I can define myself and decide if I'm loveable and valuable.*

Once I understood it's up to me, I took stock and decided that I'm just as loveable, valuable, capable and competent as everyone else. I'm different (as we all are) in the ways that make me unique, which is good. I also noticed that I'm a good person and am OK as I am.

This doesn't mean that I'm 'perfect', since there really is no such thing. I think that the definition of 'perfect' is up to each of us, and I've come to understand that I'm the 'perfect' me. This doesn't mean there isn't room for growth. It means that even with my challenges and imperfections, I can love and appreciate myself. I'm also worthy of that from others. If for some reason they don't feel that way about me, it's their problem, not mine.

I still remember how painful life was when I didn't value myself. My goal now is to support and empower others so they will never have to feel that pain.

I've learned that people who have positive self-esteem have an easier time dealing with whatever life brings them. Those who feel they have value are able to cope with life's challenges and traumas and move ahead. For those who don't love and accept themselves, everything seems to be a struggle.

I hope if you have doubts about yourself, you'll be able to re-evaluate your old beliefs and rediscover the amazing person you've always been.

What Is Self-Esteem?

SELF-ESTEEM! What is it? How do you get it? How do you *keep* it?

After much thought, experience and education, I know that you have positive self-esteem when you accept and love every part of yourself. You love the "good" parts that are kind, thoughtful, smart, talented, attractive, charming, powerful, etc. And you acknowledge and accept the parts of you that might be angry, mean, violent, rude, sloppy, ugly, grumpy and weak. You love it all, because this amazing combination of qualities is what makes you a unique human being.

Loving and accepting yourself doesn't mean that you're arrogant or think you're better than everyone else. It simply means you accept yourself, warts and all. You acknowledge that there is always room for learning and personal growth, but you don't beat yourself up all the time about your faults. You make allowances for the fact that you're still growing. (Hint: if you're alive, you're still growing. That's part of what life is all about.)

To have positive self-esteem you need to accept that you're human. This means that you take pride in your many talents, strengths and unique qualities. Since others usually support you when you're proud of your abilities and accomplishments, appreciating this part of yourself is pretty easy. However, when you have positive self-esteem you also acknowledge the parts of you that are not always perfect, positive, or socially acceptable. You have compassion for yourself as you recognize that these attributes are also part of who you are.

True self-love is nonjudgmental, which means you're familiar with and allow yourself to be all of who you are, without arrogance or shame.

It's important to note that having nonjudgmental self-love and acceptance does not mean that you are perfect or that there is no need for personal growth or improvement. It simply means that you are aware of all aspects of yourself, the ones you're satisfied with and the ones you're not, and that you accept your total self.

Over the years you've gathered incredible amounts of data about who you are. Input from the people and events in your world have helped create how you currently define your "self."

When you were born you were perfect. (All babies are perfect. Even if they have physical, mental or emotional defects, they are the best they can be, and are their perfect self.) Soon after birth you began to interpret the world around you and your place in it. You did this by watching and listening to others as they related to you and to each other.

If your parents or significant adults responded positively when you had a need (i.e. they fed you when you cried from hunger and held you when you cried for attention) you learned you were a lovable, valuable person and that your needs were important.

However, if the opposite happened, and your cries for help and comfort were ignored or met with angry voices or rough treatment, you may have interpreted this to mean that you were unimportant and that your needs didn't matter. If this happened often, you probably began to feel unimportant, rejected and valueless.

Your early interaction with your caregivers created your first concept of *self*—who you are. It began when you were a baby, and eventually grew into how you now feel about yourself. Your self-esteem today is a composite of your perception of all the input, positive and negative, verbal and nonverbal, that you've received throughout your lifetime.

The exciting thing is that, in reality, ***how others respond to you does not define who you are!*** *The responses of other people* are a reflection of who they are, and whatever is going on for them at a particular time, more than it is about you.

For example, when you were little your mother may have had a fight with her husband, and have been angry and upset when you awoke from your nap. She was not in an emotional place to deal positively with a sleepy, crying baby, so she ignored your cries for attention. You might have interpreted this to mean, "I'm not important," while in reality the problem was what was happening with your mother.

If your self-image is negative, it's probably based on many similarly incorrectly interpreted, non-verbal messages such as this.

What's important is to know that it wasn't an accurate assessment of your importance or value.

The Difference Between Self-Esteem and Self-Confidence

You might not feel good about yourself. You might be quick to negatively judge who you are. At the same time you might also feel quite confident on the job, playing a sport you excel at, or doing an activity in which you perform extremely well. This is the difference between self-confidence and self-esteem.

Self-confidence is how you think and feel about your ability to go out and do your day. Whether you believe you can accomplish a task or do an activity at any given time. Your level of confidence can be affected by a multitude of things including your current health, the people around you, your familiarity with the activity you're doing, how you feel about your appearance, the weather, and thousands of other variables. There will be some days when you feel strong and in control of your life, and your confidence will be high. There will be other days when, for various reasons your confidence is low and you'd really rather stay in bed and let someone else take care of everything.

Self-confidence is similar to a tiny boat on the ocean. It can be tossed about or sail smoothly depending on surface conditions.

Self-esteem is the acceptance, compassion and non-judgmental love you feel for the person you are, regardless of what's happening around you. It's a constant, and is not affected much by everyday events.

Self-esteem can be compared to the depths of the ocean that remain calm and unchanged even during violent storms.

While self-confidence may fluctuate daily and even hourly, it takes something huge to affect your self-esteem.

SHERI'S STORY

Sheri is smart, attractive, well educated, and very successful in her job. When she goes to work she feels strong and in control because she's worked in the same industry for 15 years and knows she'll be able to handle whatever comes up. In her professional life she is very confident.

SHERI'S STORY, CTD

However, when Sheri goes home it's a different story. You see, Sheri doesn't value who she is. She'd like to eventually get married and have children, yet she continues to date men who use her for her money, treat her poorly, and disrespect her. She doesn't respect herself so she thinks she's only good enough for men who also don't respect her. She's confused about why none of them will make a commitment.

Even though Sheri's professional self-confidence is good, her self-esteem is low. She doesn't like or respect herself, so she continues to attract and stay with men who also disrespect her.

Sheri was tired of being treated poorly and decided she'd rather be alone. She took six months to focus on herself, and started to get a positive new perspective on the woman she is. She now understands that she is as valuable in every area of her life as she is at work.

Chapter Two: Where Did I Come From?

"If the family were a fruit, it would be an orange, a circle of sections, held together but separable—each segment distinct."
—Letty Cottin Pogrebin

Family Patterns

Most parents love their children and try to do their best when raising them. One thing that parents do, both verbally and nonverbally, is to instill values, morals, beliefs and attitudes in their children. This is often done consciously, as your parents tell and teach you what has worked, or not worked, for them. Or it might be done subconsciously, as you observe them and how they function as they go through their daily lives.

Most likely the values you are taught and live by are the same values your parents learned from their parents, and ones they feel have worked well in their own lives.

Your family's value system probably included everything from table manners and the "Golden Rule," to ideas about other nationalities, law and order, and respect for self and others.

Sometimes families discuss these concepts, but very often (as with issues such as sex or money) they may never be mentioned. Nonverbal messages are just as powerful and have just as strong an influence as those that are verbalized.

If a subject is never talked about, or whenever it comes up Mom sighs and Dad raises his eyebrows, the unspoken message is that "this is an unacceptable topic; it doesn't belong in our life; nice people don't discuss/do such things," etc. When you were young you picked up innumerable parental attitudes and '*shoulds*' regarding many issues. Whether they were verbal or nonverbal, you got the message and probably incorporated them into your definition of the world without even knowing it.

'Shoulds'

A lot of these values, attitudes and beliefs become your 'shoulds'. A 'should' is something you 'know' you're supposed to do or believe, even though you may not have ever given any thought as to why! For some reason you feel if you don't follow the 'should,' it will create problems for you and those around you.

When you were young you had very little ability to meet your physical and emotional needs, and were therefore dependent upon the adults in your life to take care of you. They might have taught you to be quiet, cooperative and selfless. When they were angry or upset with you for failure to follow a 'should,' your needs probably were not met. Consequently, you quickly learned what was expected of you and what was acceptable or unacceptable behavior in your family. You learned to cooperate with such messages and expectations (usually nonverbal) without question in order to gain love and approval, get your physical and emotional needs met, and avoid rejection.

The behavior of your significant adults toward you, each other, and the world in general, created a myriad of messages from which you began to form your self-image, and on which you probably still base your own values and belief system. This belief system has become the '*shoulds*' by which you run your adult life.

These messages often manifest as your self-talk. This is the little voice in your head that tells you what to think and feel about things and how to interpret situations. At this moment it might be saying, "What! I have no such thing! Only crazy people have voices in their heads." That attitude is a 'should' you learned somewhere along the way.

If you're lucky your internal messages are positive, nonjudgmental, loving and self-supporting. If not, and your criticized and controlled by your 'shoulds', they're probably interfering with your ability to love and accept yourself. They're interfering with your ability to develop and maintain positive self-esteem.

Negative *'shoulds'* often keep you from accepting personal power, taking care of your own needs, and allowing you to love and nurture all of who you are.

You learned 'shoulds' for survival as a child. Now that you're grown they could still be part of what keeps you from being assertive and claiming your rights and personal power.

Below are a few 'shoulds' commonly accepted in current American society and which might have been part of your family values:

- "It's shameful to make mistakes."
- "If questioned you must always give an answer or explanation."
- "It's selfish to put your needs ahead of those of others."
- "People don't want to hear your feelings, so you should keep them to yourself."
- "Only weak people cry or ask for help."
- "To be loveable you have to be physically attractive."
- "Pride is a sin. Be modest and don't share your success."

Many of these 'shoulds' probably worked in your childhood to aid in meeting your needs, but no longer fit the adult you've become. The important thing is for you to be aware of the subconscious 'shoulds' that control you. Then you can see if they still support you in being a powerful adult.

Once you've looked at your 'shoulds' and identified the ones that limit you or no longer fit the person you are, you can give yourself permission to change them to meet your needs. Or you can completely let them go.

The wonderful thing is that now that you're an adult, you have the power to create the values, attitudes, and beliefs you want to live by. You may find that many of the values your parents taught you still fit your adult life and are worth keeping (things such as be reliable, responsible and trustworthy, be kind to animals and children, respect others, etc.)

However, some values, attitudes and beliefs from your childhood may have outlived their usefulness, or changed with the culture or your lifestyle choices. The exciting thing is that **you have the power to let them go** and create new values that fit who you are now.

JOSH'S STORY

When Josh was small he paid attention to his parents as they talked about their thoughts and expectations and he learned many attitudes and beliefs which he carried into adulthood. Some of these beliefs were about the role of men in our culture. He was taught that strong men don't show their feelings, and that it's shameful and unmanly to make mistakes. He learned that when you do something 'wrong' others will reject you, and that as a man he should always lead and be in control.

These attitudes (and many more) became 'shoulds' for Josh, who tried to live his life by them. The result was that Josh ignored the loving, sensitive, emotional part of himself, and presented a strong, cold front to the world.

Once he married his emotional reserve caused problems with his wife, who wanted to get close to the man she loved. In order to save his marriage Josh had to examine his 'shoulds' about being a man. In the process he discovered his beliefs might have fit for his father, but no longer worked for Josh.

Once Josh understood he had the power to create his own set of beliefs about being a man, he was able to let go of the ones from his childhood and develop attitudes that reflect who he is now.

Always remember that as an adult, **you have the power to define the rules you by which you live, who you are, and how you want to run your life.** That is your ultimate right.

"I often think you bring unhappiness on yourself, because if you don't like yourself very much, you allow yourself to be influenced by people who reinforce that."

—Lynn Johnston

"A role model in the flesh provides more than inspiration; his or her very existence is confirmation of possibilities one may have every reason to doubt, saying, 'Yes, someone like me can do this.'"

—Sonia Sotomayor

"We never know which lives we influence, or when, or why."

—Stephen King

Chapter Three: Who Influenced You?

"To free us from the expectations of others, to give us back to ourselves—there lies the great, singular power of self-respect."
—Joan Didion

"Tension is who you think you should be. Relaxation is who you are." —Chinese Proverb

Parents and Siblings

There are probably many people who have had a profound impact on the person you now are. Parents, or the adults who raised you, were the first people to teach you about the world and who you are in it. They might have done a great job, but there might also have been times when they didn't.

It's important to remember parents are people too! Most parents do their best to take good care of their children and teach them what they know about getting by in life.

When you were young you might not have thought of your parents as anything except "mom and dad," yet they filled many other roles and were individuals with their own likes, dislikes, needs, wants, and fears. The characteristics you observed in your parents were part of the building blocks in the formation of your own self-image and self-esteem.

Think about your parents or the significant adults who raised you. Who were they? What type of people were they? What individual talents and qualities did they possess? What were their challenges and fears? How do you imagine they felt about life, parenthood, marriage, and their own parents?

When you can see them as individuals, human beings with the same emotions and challenges you might now be experiencing, you'll be able to feel compassion for them. You'll also be able to appreciate them for whatever positive support they gave you, and hopefully forgive them for being human.

If you interacted with brothers or sisters, they also had an impact on your perception of the world, and may have contributed to your 'shoulds'.

Significant Others

In addition to parents and siblings, there were most likely other people in your life who profoundly influenced you. Relatives, teachers, scout leaders, religious leaders, friends, and others might have influenced you in a positive or negative way. The characteristics of these people and their interactions with you played an important part in your early development and definition of who you are.

Some of the people from your past may have become heroes or role models for you. Others might have caused you pain or self-doubt. Some people might have fallen into both categories – providing positive support in some areas and negativity in others.

Now that you're an adult it's helpful to identify the people from your past who influenced you enough to affect how you feel about yourself today.

Heroes

Who do you admire or see as a role model? These are your heroes, and might be people with special qualities or talents that you respect, people who have exhibited behaviors or performed deeds that you admire, or people who have influenced you in some way.

The people you admire could have been present in your life, or they could be people you didn't know personally, but respected for what they'd done.

Being aware of the qualities you admire in others helps you appreciate those aspects in yourself. (Yes, these characteristics are inside you, even if you don't currently see them!). This awareness also guides you as you set goals for your own personal development.

SAM'S STORY

When Sam was in grade school he was a lonely boy. He was shy and smaller than the other boys, so he became the one who was ignored or bullied.

However, Mr. Wilson, the principal at Sam's school, saw how smart and motivated Sam was, and found every opportunity to give him special tasks and empower him to be his best. He made it clear to Sam and others that he knew Sam had a lot to offer and he believed in him.

Sam is now a successful adult who stands tall and believes in himself. He remembers Mr. Wilson with much affection, for helping him gain a new perspective and start believing in himself.

Sam says that Mr. Wilson turned his life around, and will always be his hero.

Negative People

If there were people in your past, or even people in your life now, that have negatively affected you in some way, you have the right to let go of them. You can also let go of their old negative messages that might be part of your self-talk and still be running in your head.

One of the best things about being an adult is that you have the power to choose the people with whom you wish to surround yourself. You are also in control of the attitudes and beliefs you want to maintain. You can decide who makes you feel good and will cheer you on in your everyday life; and who does not support you.

Supportive and Unsupportive People

One way of being assertive is to consciously choose the people with whom you wish to surround yourself. You have the right to decide who makes you feel good and will cheer you on everyday, and to put them in your life, either physically, mentally or both. You can also note which ones do not support you in meeting your wants and needs, and avoid them physically in your daily life and mentally in how you talk to yourself.

Surrounding yourself with supportive people and ignoring those who are unsupportive, reinforces your self-confidence and helps build self-esteem.

Often people are both supportive and negative at different times or around different issues. Always know that you have the power to view these people in two ways (i.e. "positive mother" and "negative mother") and allow them in your life and in your self-talk only in the ways that are most helpful for you.

Chapter Four: Personal Power

"Lord grant me the serenity to accept the things I cannot change, the power to change the things I can, and the wisdom to know the difference." —AA Serenity prayer

WE ALL NEED to feel we have some control and personal power over the events in our lives. When you were a child this control may have been over things as small as whether you drank milk, juice, or water. As you matured, your need for personal power grew to the point where now, as an adult, you want to have the final say in almost everything that affects you.

At times, however, other peoples' need for power and control may overwhelm your own, prompting you to give away your individual rights for the sake of peace and harmony, or to feel loved and appreciated (as you did as a child).

When this happens you might feel resentful, bitter, taken advantage of, angry, and vulnerable. If experienced often, these unpleasant emotions can erode your self-esteem and undermine your personal growth.

It's common to make the mistake of trying to regain control by focusing on changing those around you. This is usually a futile exercise, and one that will end in your feeling anxious and frustrated. The reality is, ***the only person you have control over is yourself***.

The term for trying to change your life by changing others is co-dependence. When you act in a co-dependent way you're putting yourself in a victim role, since the victim stance is one of being powerless. If you find yourself saying "Everything would be fine if only he or she would ___," it's a sign you've given away your power and are concentrating on changing the wrong person.

To Reclaim Your Power

You can regain the feelings of strength and power by taking charge of the situation and looking at what you can do or change to affect it. Find what you have control over, and do something about that. Sometimes that means stating your ideas, feelings, and needs, with the expectation they will be met. Sometimes it means removing yourself from the situation. Either way, you will be exerting your personal power, taking charge of the situation, and valuing yourself. When you do this, you will be claiming your power and begin improving your self-esteem.

Even if the other person refuses to meet your needs, you can still take care of yourself by changing how you view the situation and what you expect, or by removing yourself from it. Your perception and definition of a situation sets the tone for the way you choose to deal with it.

Here are some steps you can take to maintain your personal power and strength:

1. Look at all options available to you and decide if it's possible to have an impact on the situation.

2. If you have determined that it's possible to have an impact, then state your thoughts, feelings, and needs clearly to yourself and others.

3 Stay unemotional and don't allow others to sidetrack you or belittle what you're saying.

4. Remove yourself from the situation, or if you choose to keep things as they are, accept responsibility for that decision.

5. If you truly have no control over the situation, then redefine it for yourself and see what other options are available to you.

It's a good idea to look at areas in your life where you feel in control and strong, and areas where you are feeling victimized because you may have purposefully or inadvertently given away your personal rights and power.

Take a few minutes to think about when you feel strong and powerful, and when you feel at the mercy of others. Also, pay attention to how your body reacts when you're feeling in control of a situation and when you don't (ie: relaxed and comfortable or clenched jaw and tense muscles). Then decide what you'd like to do about it.

AMBER'S STORY

Amber was raised in a controlling family where her every move was dictated. She had to comply or risk emotional rejection or physical consequences. As a result Amber grew up believing it was safest to allow other people to control her life.

When she married it was to someone who was as controlling as her family had been. Soon after the wedding she realized she was miserable and tired of being victimized. Her life wasn't coming together as she wanted, and she began to see that as an adult she had the right to be in charge of herself.

She started going to a counselor who helped her see she has rights and the ability to make her own choices. She began to reclaim her power by taking control and being in charge of her decisions and her life.

Amber now lives according to her own beliefs and always considers her needs and wishes when making decisions.

Passive, Assertive and Aggressive Behavior

Passive. Assertive. Aggressive. You've probably heard these words but you might not be familiar with their meaning or how they fit into your life.

All three words refer to modes of behavior and ways of approaching and dealing with life. You act in a *passive* manner when you choose to ignore or suppress your own needs in order to meet the needs of others. As we've mentioned, for the convenience of others you might have been taught to be passive as a child. In return for being quiet, "not rocking the boat," not "making waves," and being cooperative and undemanding, the significant adults in your life met your physical needs, and hopefully your emotional needs as well. It was a bargain: when you were a good boy or girl, they made you feel valuable, lovable, and safe. In the process, you may have learned to be passive.

Being passive involves giving away your personal power and trusting others to meet your needs. Sometimes it works and sometimes it doesn't. One thing passivity does is it slowly erodes your self-esteem and sense of being a capable, competent person.

Take Jason for example. As a child he was raised to always be cooperative and never say no to others. Now, as a 34-year old adult, he has trouble standing up for himself. When a coworker asks him to cover for her and work an extra shift, Jason says, "OK, I guess so, if you really need me." He gives this response even though he already has plans that he now has to cancel. He chooses to be passive and meet the needs of another at the expense of his own.

You act *assertively* when you choose to stand up for yourself without attacking or putting down another person. You make a conscious choice to take responsibility for meeting your own needs, while also choosing to not take away the rights of another in the process. Assertive behavior enhances your sense of personal power and self-esteem.

If Jason had chosen to respond assertively when asked to work late, he could have said, "No, I'm sorry that I can't. It's not convenient for me tonight." This response would have met his needs without attacking or harming his coworker.

Aggressive action is choosing to meet your own needs at the expense of another, or when you purposefully attack or demean another in the process of taking care of yourself. Aggressive behavior temporarily increases your sense of personal power, but decreases your self-esteem.

Back to Jason. He could have acted aggressively by saying, "Absolutely not! I can't believe you're so lazy as to leave early and expect others to cover for you! I'll never understand why you were hired in the first place!" With this response Jason would certainly have made his point that he wasn't free to work, but also unnecessarily attacked his coworker in the process.

We all have moments when we act in each of these three ways. However, the healthiest and most conducive to personal growth is to be assertive most of the time.

When you choose to act assertively, the people in our life may initially resent their loss of control over you, or be angry that you're now putting yourself first and them second. They might try to make you feel guilty about your behavior, and label you as selfish, inconsiderate, unsympathetic, and uncaring. Their goal is to evoke guilt so you will stop whatever you are doing to take care of yourself and resume taking care of them.

It's important for you to know which people in your life try to control you with guilt and suffering whenever you become assertive. It's also important to know that *you have a right to take care of yourself and meet your needs.* Give yourself permission to do this regardless of the reactions of others.

You might find it helpful to look at the people and situations in your life and identify where you act in each of these three ways. If you're not happy with the outcome, choose a situation, act assertively, and see what happens and how you feel.

KIM'S STORY

Kim was raised believing 'good women' are sweet, cooperative and passive. Her mother exemplified this behavior, except when she 'snapped' and lashed out in anger at whoever was around. Her mother taught Kim to be both passive and aggressive, neither of which are healthy behaviors.

When Mom was passive her needs were ignored and everyone pushed her around. When she was aggressive she hurt and frightened people. Kim didn't want to do either of these, but realized that she was acting just like mom.

As a child Kim didn't know about being assertive, but once she learned the concept she realized it was the most effective way to act. Kim now asks herself, "What do I want in this situation?" and then deals assertively with others to make it happen. She finds that this works best for her.

Chapter Five: Relationships

THE WAY YOU INTERACT with people influences, and is influenced by, the way you feel about yourself. You first learned how to relate to others by watching and listening to your parents, grandparents, siblings, and friends. You observed how they talked with you and each other, and began to recognize patterns of relating that felt good and patterns that did not. You also learned which behaviors helped you get along with people and which ones got you into "big trouble."

When you were young you were probably taught to seek approval from adults by behaving in certain ways. You most likely tried to act in the ways that brought the most rewards.

As an adolescent wanting approval from your peers, you picked up clues from your friends about what worked best in talking to people of your same sex and people of the opposite sex. Your self-confidence may have grown and shrunk according to the way you perceived interactions with your friends.

Now that you're an adult, the good news is that you no longer need to seek approval from anyone outside yourself! You can behave and interact with people in ways that enhance you both. You can choose to be around people who are positive, honest with you and themselves.

You might find it helpful to look back to when you were a child and adolescent, and remember how interacting with others felt for you then.

Notice if these feelings and behaviors still form the basis for your interactions with men, women, and authority figures today.

Ask yourself if this mode of behavior meets your current needs as an adult. Is there something you would like to do differently?

If you discover you're still connecting with people as you did when you were young, even though doing so is not representative of the powerful, confident person you are today, know you have the power to change your behavior at any time.

Intimacy

The dictionary defines intimacy as a close, familiar, usually loving or affectionate personal relationship. Your ability to achieve and maintain intimacy is directly proportional to your level of self-esteem.

Creating intimacy with another takes time and care. It begins slowly and "safely," by talking and listening, sharing common interests, and developing mutual trust and respect.

As time goes on the two people involved begin to trust each other, and as a result begin to share on a deeper, more personal level. If this sharing of oneself is received in a kind, caring, nonjudgmental manner, then eventually each of you will be willing to risk being "the real you," and reveal those aspects you consider to be your vulnerabilities and flaws.

As long as the slow revelation of the whole personality is treated with respect and care, intimacy can be developed and maintained. However, if either person betrays that trust, the development of intimacy may be interrupted, stopped, or damaged.

People who have healthy self-esteem are usually more willing and able to take the risk of slowly revealing who they are, and to be non-judgmental with others.

Some of the qualities that exist in an intimate relationship are:

- Respect
- Trust
- Emotional and Physical Safety
- Honesty

- Laughter and Humor
- Sharing Your History
- Kindness
- Ability to Safely be Vulnerable

- Acceptance of Differences
- Physical Affection
- Appreciation
- Communication/both Listening and Talking

JIM'S STORY

Jim was raised in a family where things were promised and then never delivered on, so he learned he couldn't trust the people he loved to do what they said they would.

Now that he's an adult trust is still a big issue for Jim. He wants to feel close to his wife and friends, but has trouble believing when they tell him something.

His mistrust was causing problems with his marriage and impeding his ability to feel emotionally safe and intimate with his wife. When he realized this, he talked with her about his vulnerability around trust and his need for her to be consistent with follow through when she promised to do something. As a result she is very careful to follow through when she can and let him know when she can't. Jim now feels safe enough to be intimate and is beginning to learn to trust.

You may want to ask yourself, "Which qualities of intimacy are easy for me to achieve and which do I struggle with?" If you choose to, you can decide to develop the qualities that are getting in the way of you forming intimate relationships.

"The most influential and frequent voice you hear is your inner-voice. It can work in your favor or against you, depending on what you listen to and act upon."

—Maddy Malhotra

"As you stumble and learn, stumble and learn again, resolve to talk to yourself as if you were your best friend."

—Timothy Ferriss

"It's not who you are that holds you back. It's who you think you're not."

—Anonymous

Chapter Six: Thoughts

The Shadow

One key element of positive self-esteem is acceptance and compassion for all aspects of your personality. Not merely for the part of yourself that is "the good little girl or boy," the part who follows all the 'shoulds,' but also for the aspects of your personality that you might want to hide, even from yourself.

If you came from a family that rejected or punished you when certain aspects of your personality appeared, you probably learned to hide these aspects because you were taught that having them is shameful and makes you unlovable.

Many years ago psychologist Carl Jung developed the concept of The Shadow. He explained that we all have a Shadow, which is everything we like to think we're not. According to Jung, your Shadow is the hidden and repressed aspects of your personality. This includes all the negative conclusions you drew about yourself during childhood, all the unpleasant feelings and thoughts that go against your 'shoulds' and label you as incompetent, unlovable, and worthless.

Jung divided our personality into three sections and visualized them as a series of circles, one inside the other.

YOUR FAÇADE   YOUR SHADOW   YOUR REAL SELF

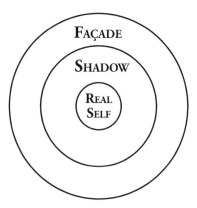

Facade

The outermost circle is your Facade. This is the part of yourself that you most often choose to share with the world. This is the nice, polite, fun, happy attractive, intelligent, cooperative part. It's also the part you want to believe is the total you, since it gains you the most love, acceptance, and positive feedback from others. It's the part of yourself you use to gain a sense of worth. Fortunately it's only one aspect of the complete person you really are.

Shadow

The middle circle is The Shadow. Your Shadow is unlovable, flawed, incompetent, angry, violent, cruel, grumpy, stupid, selfish, and uncooperative. It's everything you'd like to think you're not. Your Shadow is ugly and you may fear that if you acknowledge it, it will define who you are.

You were probably taught that this part of yourself is bad, and that people will reject you if they see it. As a result you might live in terror of others seeing through your Facade to your dark, black, embarrassing, feelings. However, it's important to understand that The Shadow is as essential to all of who you are as your Facade is, and that it *is not your identity!* The Shadow does not define who you are, just as your Facade does not. It's only a part of the incredible whole.

As long as you're afraid to confront the unpleasant aspect of your personality, this fear will control you. You will spend a lot of time, energy, and money trying to ignore or deny part of your being. It's exhausting!

However, when you finally allow yourself to get in touch with EVERY aspect of your personality, you will find it incredibly freeing. Once you confront your darkest fears about yourself, those fears will lose their power and you will be moving along the road to complete self-acceptance, compassion, and acknowledgment of your Real Self.

Acknowledging your Shadow does not mean allowing it to run rampant, harming yourself and others. It means accepting that it's there, and working with it instead of trying to ignore it or deny its existence.

Acknowledging your Shadow also means you that don't reject parts of yourself. Instead you accept that you are human, and that you experience all emotions at various times.

The way to release yourself from your Shadow's grip is to accept it as part of who you are. Some people find it helpful to write down their Shadow aspects. Once you've faced them and they are no longer secret, they lose their power.

Once acknowledged, the power of your Shadow will diminish and you can then work with it. When it appears you can say to yourself, "Oh, there's that angry part of me. What will I choose to do with it?" instead of saying, "It's not OK for me to be angry because I'm a nice person, nice people don't get angry, so I won't allow it."

Denying part of yourself is stressful and unproductive. It's important to accept all parts of who you are and realize that your Shadow doesn't define you. It's just a part of the incredible whole that makes you unique.

Your Real Self

The innermost circle represents Your Real Self, which is the combination of all parts of your personality: the positive and negative, good and evil, gifts and talents and all aspects that go into making you the unique human being you are. Once you recognize your Real Self you will no longer feel the need to maintain a Façade, believe other people's 'shoulds' or deny your Shadow. With the knowledge, acceptance and compassion for your total self, you will at last be able to relax and enjoy all parts of yourself.

MIKE'S STORY

Mike's Shadow was always lurking in the back of his mind. Even when he was doing something he was proud of, he knew there was another part of him that wasn't so great. His fear of this part of his personality interfered with his ability to accept and appreciate himself. Mike thought that if he wasn't perfect, then he was seriously flawed and not loveable, valuable or acceptable.

As we all do, Mike had a dark side to his personality. Because of his early training he chose to define himself by the negative side and ignore the positive.

Whenever one of his 'shadow' thoughts or behaviors appeared he would use it as proof that he was defective.

Mike forgot that all people have two sides, the 'good' and the negative, and that both sides are important because together they create the whole unique person he is.

The perfection he strove for is impossible to achieve, because he is human, and human beings are balanced with both 'good' and 'bad'. Mike had forgotten that it's vital for him to accept the parts of himself he doesn't like rather than run from them.

When Mike began to look at and accept his Shadow as part of himself, he could then make decisions about how he wanted to work with it. He stopped running from it, accepted himself, flaws and all, and was able to acknowledge his Shadow and make behavior choices which took away it's power.

Self-Talk—The Little Voice in Your Head

"Life is 10% what happens to me and 90% how I choose to react to it." —Charles Swindall

You may have noticed there's a "little voice" in your head that provides running commentary on all that's happening. This voice is the narrator of your life, and is constantly interpreting events for you (even at this very moment, as you read this, it might be saying, "What in the world are they talking about? I have no such thing!"). This voice provides *self-talk,* and is an extremely powerful force because it creates your feelings!

"What?" you ask! "Aren't I at the mercy of my feelings, which just happen by themselves?" The answer is a resounding "NO!" Feelings do not just happen, because situations do not come with emotions attached.

Feelings come after your little voice, based on your values, attitudes, and beliefs, has interpreted and defined a situation for you. This interpretation creates a perception, which then lets you know how to feel!

For example, a mother may try to make creative, yummy lunches for her two school-age children. She probably does this because one of her 'shoulds' about being a 'good mother' is that a good mom provides nutritious lunches for her kids. She hopes that her kids will know this, and love and appreciate her for her efforts.

Her son, who believes the same 'should', interprets his mother's actions to mean that she loves and provides for him. However, her daughter sees the wonderful lunches as an affront to her independence. Her perception and self-talk say, "My mother must think I don't know how to take care of myself, or even choose what I want to eat, so she does it for me."

Consequently, the daughter is angry at, and resentful of, her mom for not believing she can take care of herself and allowing her to be more self-sufficient.

Notice these are **two different reactions to the same action**. The only difference is that each person interpreted the situation in his or her own way, and the little voice then let each know how to feel! (This is also why it's impossible to please everyone, all the time. Regardless of your intent, the individual interpretations of your actions are beyond your control).

It's quite liberating to know your feelings are the result of your self-talk, because then you can be in charge of whether you are happy, sad, optimistic, self-confident, angry, content, or whatever. *You are in charge of your feelings rather than at their mercy!* How you define a situation and what you say to yourself about it will create your feelings.

HEATHER'S STORY

Heather noticed she had a little voice in her head that narrated her life. She knew she wasn't crazy, since in a moment of honesty her girlfriend shared that she did too. Heather didn't know that it was her self-talk, which is something we all have.

Heather was aware that the voice continuously described and judged her thoughts, feelings and actions. It had been there as long as she could remember, so she assumed it must be right. Consequently she believed it and allowed it to control her.

Occasionally the voice would tell Heather she was doing well, but more often it would criticize and tell her that she was flawed, making mistakes, and was doomed to fail. It also told her what to think, feel and believe about others.

Sometimes she agreed with what the voice was saying, like "obey the law", "do a good job", or "be kind to people." At other times the voice told her what she should think and how she should feel, and the message didn't fit the adult she'd become. When that happened Heather felt conflicted if she followed her desires and chose to do something that went against what the voice was telling her.

Heather didn't realize that the voice was really the voices of hundreds of people from her past. Over the years she had incorporated their thoughts, attitudes and beliefs into her own, and then continued to replay them in her head.

When Heather went into counseling she began to understand where the voice came from. Once she learned about self-talk she realized that she was in control of it and had the power to change it if she didn't like it's message.

Eventually Heather was able to begin challenging the messages and make her own decisions about which ones to follow and which ones to change. She gained control of her self-talk instead of allowing it to control her, and is now comfortable with her internal dialogue.

The first step to being aware of your self-talk is to start listening and paying attention to the little voice in your head. If you don't like its message, you have the power to interrupt it and CHANGE IT, thereby changing your feelings.

You might find it helpful to take a few minutes and pay attention to your self-talk. Most likely you're telling yourself things that are creating feelings. It's fun to experiment by changing your self-talk to something different and notice how your feelings and mood shift.

If you've identified some common negative messages you often give yourself, turn those into positive affirmations. For example, if you tell yourself you don't deserve something (money, love, appreciation, respect, and so on), change that refrain into a positive one by telling yourself you're a valuable human being and that you do deserve it. Then notice the difference in how you feel.

This process of becoming aware of your self-talk and shifting it may be slow. Be patient with yourself (remember compassion), and continue to recognize your negative trigger thoughts.

Chapter Seven: Feelings

"Let's not forget that the little emotions are the great captains of our lives and we obey them without realizing it."
—Vincent Van Gogh, 1889

"Feelings are everywhere -- be gentle." *—Masai, J*

WE ALL HAVE FEELINGS. It's part of being human. Just about everyone is capable of feeling and expressing emotion, although for various reasons many may choose to suppress this vital aspect of him/herself.

The great news is that situations don't come with feelings attached. You create your feelings about something by what you tell yourself (your self-talk), your perception of what's happening. This is terrific because it means you have the power to redefine a situation and therefore create new feelings about it.

For example, Kim was staying in a relationship that didn't make her happy because she didn't want to deal with having to break up with her boyfriend, even though she knew he wasn't good for her. He decided he wasn't happy either and broke up with her. At first she was devastated because she told herself she couldn't live without him. Of course, this self-talk created feelings of fear, insecurity and panic.

However, after a couple of months she realized that her life was much happier without him and she was doing fine on her own. Her perception of the situation, and resulting self-talk, changed to being positive and excited about all the good things her future could hold.

Please note that Kim's situation stayed the same—the boyfriend was gone. The only thing that changed was her perception and the resulting self-talk, which created a whole different set of feelings.

Feelings are important because they help you identify and express what's going on inside of you. Your feelings are vital to your emotional growth and maturation, and are often a reflection of your level of self-esteem.

American culture has a lot of rules and 'shoulds' about feelings. Little boys are taught that men don't cry; they must be strong and refrain from showing any weakness. Consequently, American males often turn hurt, fear, or insecurity into anger, which society says is acceptable for men to express. On the other hand, little girls are encouraged to cry and act weak or afraid, but are discouraged from feeling and acting strong, self-confident, powerful, assertive, or angry. These emotions are considered unfeminine.

At some point you were probably told you "should" or "should not" feel some particular way. Whatever you were feeling was treated as irrelevant! You weren't "supposed to" feel a certain way, so you were taught to suppress and ignore it.

When you were told to discount or ignore what you knew was happening inside of you, you might have been confused and started to doubt yourself. After all, if the adults or authority figures in your life were telling you one thing, but you felt another, you may have decided to believe them (since they were in charge). So you stopped trusting yourself and began ignoring what you knew.

The reality is that there are no 'shoulds' around feelings. ***All feelings are normal and OK***. You always have the right to feel whatever you wish to feel. Nobody can tell you whether a feeling is correct, because there is no such thing as appropriate feelings. Whatever you feel in response to a situation is true for you.

However, even though you have the right to feel whatever you want, you DO NOT always have the right to act out those feelings. If you're feeling angry and betrayed, as Kim did in the story above, and want to do something violent in retaliation, it is not OK! It's important to understand that feelings and actions don't always have to go together! You can feel any way you wish in any situation, but it *is **not*** appropriate to act any way you wish. Our prisons are filled with people who weren't able to make that distinction.

Once you act, you're imposing your feelings on others and forcing them to deal with your emotions. For example, young parents may be dealing with a baby who is teething and has been crying for three nights in a row. They are exhausted, frustrated, angry, and desperate to get some sleep. They may also feel insecure and inadequate about their parenting skills, and wish to give that baby away to the first person who walks by: anything to achieve the peace, quiet and rest they so desperately need. Of course, even though they may feel this way, they do not actually act on these feelings by giving the child away.

Families often have many rules and expectations about feelings. They might have taught you to ignore them completely, or only acknowledge certain 'acceptable' ones. You might find it helpful to spend some time looking at the rules your family taught you about feelings, and deciding you want to keep or change them in your adult life.

If you were raised by people who didn't support you when you expressed your feelings, you might not be aware of or have words for all the emotions you feel. You can probably identify basic emotions such as happy, sad, afraid and angry, but are stuck when it comes to defining your feelings in more depth. To help you with feeling identification, we've created a list of common feelings (in no particular order) for you look over and use to begin identifying your emotions:

Happy	Proud
Sad	Stupid
Angry	Excited
Depressed	Helpless
Hurt	Devastated
Rejected	Embarrassed

Afraid	Confident
Lonely	Strong
Silly	Overwhelmed
Envious/Jealous	Betrayed
Powerless	Worthless
Ignored	Abandoned
Alone	Lost
Frustrated	Thrilled
Powerless	Powerful
Ashamed	Insignificant
Incompetent	Courageous

Since feelings follow thoughts (see section on Self-Talk), it might be beneficial for you to look at specific situations, identify your perception of them, and see which feelings are associated.

The great news is that because thoughts create your feelings, once you've identified a situation and accompanying emotions, you then have the power to redefine the event and change what you tell yourself about it, which will change your mood and feelings.

MATT'S STORY

Matt has trouble allowing himself to express his feelings. He comes from a place where the only feelings men are expected to express are major self-confidence, mild happiness or anger. In reality Matt is worried about his future, isn't sure he'll be able to support himself, and is afraid that he'll never find a woman who will love him enough to marry him.

Matt buys into the attitudes of his peer group,

which tell him that 'real men' are strong, can handle anything, should never show weakness, and aren't afraid. Therefore he doesn't allow himself to feel his fear or share it with anyone. He covers his fear with anger (which is socially acceptable in his group), and is now miserable because he's angry all the time, and is still afraid.

Matt's sister has been able to see beneath his anger, and is now supporting him as he tries to get in touch with his feelings. This is difficult for Matt because it goes against his 'macho image' and is a challenge because he's been out of touch with himself for so long that he doesn't have words to describe his emotions. However, he's realizing that his fears will become reality unless he learns to get past his fear of feelings. With his sister's help he's learning to do this.

Empathy and Compassion

Compassion is caring about, understanding and feeling empathy for the suffering of others, and is a necessary part of any good relationship. Having compassion implies that you're being supportive and fairly non-judgmental. You're focusing more on how to support the person, and possibly alleviate their pain, than on blaming or judging.

We usually think of having compassion for other people, but it's important that you also apply it to yourself. When you feel compassion for others it means that you understand and accept who they are without judgment or blame. You're aware of and acknowledge the positive and negative aspects of the whole person, and love and accept that person as she or he is.

You might find you're easily able to feel and express compassion for others, but have a more difficult time doing it for yourself.

An important part of having and keeping positive self-esteem is the ability to love, accept and want the best for yourself. Even if you believe you are flawed, you can still love yourself in a nonjudgmental way. Parents love their children when they are not perfect, and similarly, you have to love and accept yourself unconditionally if you want to have positive self-esteem.

This doesn't mean there's no room for growth or improvement. There will always be aspects of your personality you may wish to strengthen and/or change. Nonjudgmental love for yourself means that you accept all of who you are, negatives as well as positives, and love the whole.

When you were a child you may have been taught that behaviors, attitudes, feelings, things, and people are either "good" or "bad" (this is a judgment). You might have learned to judge, and then accept or reject someone or something depending on that judgment.

If an action were judged to be "good," then it was acceptable and the person who performed it was OK. However, if an action was judged as "bad," then not only was the behavior rejected, but the person who performed it was probably also labeled "bad," and rejected too. No compassion or understanding was involved, and there was no separating the person from the action, just lots of judgment.

If you were taught to view the world in this manner, you probably treat others this way, and might be even tougher on yourself. It's common for you to have learned to make allowances for the flaws and foibles of others, but for some reason be tougher on yourself.

For example, if you make a mistake or poor decision, instead of being gentle with yourself and saying, "I did the best I could and am still a capable, competent, valuable person," or "I've learned a valuable lesson which will help me in the future", you might reject your entire being along with the decision you made. You could abuse yourself with labels such as "stupid, inadequate, incompetent, and worthless," and focus on regret.

The compassionate response when you make a mistake is to "give yourself a break," know you did the best you could at the time with the information and resources available to you, and learn from the situation, rather than reject your entire self because of it.

If you deal with yourself in a very judgmental, non-compassionate way, without allowing any room for mistakes or normal human error or weakness, you will have a difficult time maintaining positive self-esteem

Always remember that having *compassion for yourself is what self-esteem is all about!*

You might find it helpful to look at your attitudes about compassion and judgment. Spend some time thinking about the situations in which you become judgmental, and what purpose that judgment serves. Also notice who you judge and who you have compassion for.

ANNE'S STORY

Anne thought of herself as a compassionate person. Whenever one of her friends had a problem she felt deeply for them, and was always the first there with flowers and support. She could feel their pain, and was proud of herself for being able to support and love them regardless of what they were going through.

However, when it came to herself Anne wasn't so compassionate. She often berated herself when she made a mistake, and was seldom as gentle with herself as she was with her friends.

Anne was horrified when her good friend pointed out that although she was good to others she was mean to herself. At first she denied it, since this didn't fit with her self-image as a compassionate person. However, she started to notice how often she used her self-talk to beat herself up, and realized that this was not compassionate behavior.

Anne hadn't understood that compassion is as important to give to herself as it is to give to others. She started paying attention to how she treated herself, made some changes, and is now focusing on being as kind and gentle to herself as she is to others. She's been surprised to notice that when she's compassionate to herself she feels good about who she is and her outlook on life is more joyful.

Fear

Fear is a normal part of life that appears when you feel vulnerable and powerless. In certain circumstances fear is a good thing because it triggers the fight, flight or freeze response designed to keep you safe in dangerous situations. Fear can also be a good motivator and help you move ahead when you're feeling stuck. However, when fear is out of control it can cause you to feel overwhelmed, depressed, and incapable of action.

We've all experienced fear. When you were young you might have been afraid of the scary monsters you thought lived in your closet or under your bed, or bigger things like being abandoned, rejected, or not being good enough to be liked or loved.

Now that you're an adult, you might still experience some of your fears from childhood. Although you are probably OK with the scary monsters under the bed, you might have brought emotional fears such as rejection or abandonment with you into adulthood. You also might fear failure or success, being alone, being seen as inadequate, the unknown, loss of control, and a wide variety of other things you don't know how to deal with.

If you allow them to, all of these fears have the power to control your behavior, and can obstruct your ability to be your happy, effective self.

Fear comes from thoughts about your seeming inability to

control a situation. Your goal is to keep yourself emotionally and physically safe, so focusing on your inadequacies, failures, or inability to be worthy or cope, allows fear to appear.

Fear, and the resulting stress and anxiety, can trigger bodily responses and physical symptoms. Common physical reactions to fear and anxiety include increased adrenaline, shortness of breath, sweaty palms, inability to hear, think or focus, increased heart rate, mental or emotional distraction, and the desire to escape.

The problem with fear is that it creeps up and lurks in the back of your mind. Then, at unexpected times, when you're at your most vulnerable, it surfaces, grips your thoughts, and directs or dictates your emotions and behaviors.

Looking honestly at fear is difficult because acknowledging it often brings up extremely painful emotions. The pain originates from having to admit to yourself or others that you're not always strong and powerful, that you are sometimes vulnerable. Consequently, recognizing and dealing with your fears requires courage, inner strength and strong self-esteem.

The good news about fear is that you can confront it, and once you do, it will no longer control you. Fear only has power over you when you try to ignore it or run from it. The harder you run and the more effort you put into ignoring whatever is frightening you, the stronger and more powerful it will become.

However, once you stop running and face the fear, its power to intimidate and control you will diminish or disappear. Taking action will get rid of your fear. Try it and see how it works for you.

Here are some steps to help you deal with your fears.

1. Think about your fear. What, specifically is it?

2. State your fear aloud, write it, or talk about it with others.

3. Ask yourself, "How valid is this fear?" and determine if there is really something to be afraid of.

4. Look at the ways your fears inhibit or alter your behavior. Do they prevent you from being who you really are?

5. Ask yourself if you would be able to cope or survive if what you fear turned into reality?

6. Create a plan to put your fears in perspective so they no longer interfere with who you are?

SARAH'S STORY

Sarah is afraid of a lot of things. She fears physical things like water (even showers and water on her head), and falling. She's also afraid of emotional things such as making a mistake and being rejected or hurt because of it.

Some of these fears came from events in her childhood and some just appeared over the years for no particular reason. Unfortunately, because of her fears Sarah has severely limited her life. She's afraid to go out and do much, and is allowing her fears to dictate her behavior.

As she lived her fears Sarah noticed how narrow and boring her life had become. She was unhappy with this so decided to change it. She looked realistically at the things she was afraid of, and realized that most of them didn't have much validity.

Since she was tired of her life being run by fear Sarah decided to challenge the voice in her head that told her to be fearful (her self-talk) and to look at the reality of its message. If she determined that the fear was ungrounded (like drowning in the shower), she gathered her courage, took a deep breath, and moved toward the fear rather than running from it.

After walking through the fear a couple of times it lost it's power over her.

Now she's excited to find that her world is opening up because once she faced her fears they diminished in size and no longer control her.

Remember, fear loses its power when you confront it in some way. Take some time to reflect on your ability to control your self-talk, thoughts, and feelings, and therefore, your fears.

If facing your fear won't kill or physically harm you or someone else, then make a plan to confront it. Allow yourself to **feel and confront the fear and do it anyway!**

This process will allow you to open up and be honest with yourself about your fears. Once you do you will feel relief, your anxiety level will drop, and you will be able to put your fear back into a realistic perspective and move ahead.

Anger

You're probably familiar with anger. It's the feeling that pops up when you think someone has in some way harmed you or another. Your life might be going along smoothly, and then something happens and suddenly you're grinding your teeth, clinching your jaw or fists, feeling flushed, taking shallow breaths, and preparing to yell or fight.

Anger comes from your perception of a situation, which is usually the result of negative self-talk, in which you define circumstances in a negative way.

At times, anger is appropriate. It can be helpful because it increases your adrenaline, which triggers your natural fight or flight response and enables you to defend yourself if necessary. However, anger is often misplaced and can cause you to think poorly or analyze a situation inaccurately. You might lash out in anger when another action would have been a more productive choice.

Anger can be a "cover-up" emotion. This means there may be other, more vulnerable feelings beneath the anger. If you are fearful, have poor self-esteem, often relive old hurts, feel insecure, ashamed, are afraid of being rejected, disrespected, invalidated, or powerless, you might turn those feelings into anger and verbally or physically attack someone.

If you choose to express your anger by lashing out at others or yourself, becoming aggressive, hurtful or violent, then anger is a problem for you.

JENNIFER'S STORY

Last week Jen was driving down Main Street when a car full of rowdy teenage boys passed her and one of them flipped her off. Her response to this was instant rage. Her first inclination was to chase them down and make them pay for their rudeness.

Fortunately, Jen realized her reaction was out of line with what had happened, and that it probably reflected more about her than about the boys.

As she looked at the situation she realized that as a child she was often judged, treated rudely and rejected by people who didn't even know her (like the teenage boys). This current incident brought back the pain of those earlier experiences.

Once Jen understood where her rage came from she was able to put it in perspective, change her self-talk about it, let the anger go, and actually laugh at the absurdity of the boy's action.

Understanding what triggers your anger can help you become aware of your vulnerabilities. Once you identify these more vulnerable emotions and understand what kinds of things prompt them, then you can monitor your cover-up anger and deal with it by choosing a more appropriate response.

Most of the time, the challenge of anger is dealing with it in an appropriate way that will take care of you while refraining from harming the other person.

To work with your anger it's important to listen to your self-talk and understand your true feelings. Then, look at your perception of the situation and see how true it is.

You might find it helpful to look at where you tend to lose control or become angry and identify the things or people in your life that push these buttons. Choose several situations, identify what you were really feeling, and which emotions you were covering up. Doing so allows you to create new options for handling those situations the next time they arise.

Frustration

When you feel powerless or out of control, you may say you are frustrated. Frustration is what I call a "red flag" emotion. The 'red flags' let you know that something else is going on for you.

Frustration's job is to let you know you're in a situation over which you have no power or control. The circumstances may be such that you have to wait for others to make decisions or take action, or they have made decisions that affect you in a negative way. Or you're trying to control people or things and they're not being cooperative so it's not working as you planned.

Frustration is a signal you've lost your sense of personal power. It's an indication you're feeling blocked or stuck in some way, powerless over events and what's happening to you. This kind of situation can shake your self-confidence and cause anger or depression. Rather than acknowledge and deal with your anger, depression or other uncomfortable feelings, you just 'get frustrated,' and lash out at others or abuse yourself.

A common situation that incites frustration is one that has you trying to control someone else. It might be the clerk at the store who isn't paying attention to you, the government and politicians you think aren't running the country correctly, or your children, spouse, or friends who may be making decisions you don't agree with.

In political situations there are some things you can do, such as vote, write, call your representatives, or volunteer your time and energy for your cause. At work you can talk with people to make your thoughts known and work with your boss to rally support for your ideas. However, if after exhausting those options the situation doesn't change, you might continue to focus on your apparent powerlessness and will remain frustrated.

In personal situations and relationships you might think you know what's best for another, and put lots of time and energy into trying to change or 'help' that person. However, if the object of our attention doesn't want to change, then you have no control over their choices or behavior. This can be difficult to accept, especially if you see someone making harmful choices and you just want to save them from pain and 'help' them 'get it right.'

MARK'S STORY

Mark was frustrated. His adult daughter, Christi, was dating a guy he didn't like, and Mark was concerned about where it might lead. He shared his fears with Christi, who was respectful but said she would continue to see this man.

Mark wanted to 'make her stop' so he could protect her from eventual heartache, but since she was an adult there was nothing more he could do. So he felt frustrated.

Mark realized that his frustration was an indication of his powerlessness in the situation. He also understood that to get rid of the frustration he had to find a way to reclaim his sense of power.

Since he couldn't control Christi's choices, he decided to stay close to her, try to be nonjudgmental, and let her know he loved and supported her even if he disliked her actions.

By taking control of his own feelings and behavior he was able to let go of his need to control hers, so he could maintain their relationship and be there for her when she needed him.

The bottom line in situations where you feel frustrated is that you have two choices:

1. If it's a circumstance over which you have some power and control, you can take action on your own to modify the situation in some way.

2. If it's a situation in which you have no power, you can decide it's not worth putting energy into and let it go.

The Alcoholics Anonymous Serenity Prayer says it best:

"God grant me the serenity
To accept the things I cannot change,
The courage to change the things I can,
And the wisdom to know the difference."

Allowing things to frustrate you only drains your emotional and physical energy, confuses your thoughts, creates worry (which is another useless emotion) and blocks you from feeling good and being productive.

If you want to manage your frustration the first thing to do is identify what situations cause you to feel powerless. Then think of the Serenity Prayer and truthfully answer whether you have the power and authority to affect the situation. If you do have both the responsibility and authority to make a difference, then do it. If you don't, then LET IT GO!!!

Envy and Jealousy

Envy and jealousy are feelings of rivalry between you and another person. If you envy someone it means you want the same circumstances or possessions they have. If you feel jealous, you not only want what they have, but you also want them to not have it.

JAY'S STORY

Eric & Jay each owned a deli a few blocks apart. Eric's Deli was successful and always had people coming and going, while business at Jay's Deli was pretty slow. When Jay realized this he became angry at Eric for "stealing all his business". The more he thought about it the more jealous he became, and the more he let his business slide because all his energy was going towards resenting Eric's success.

Eventually Jay realized that he was wasting his time and energy being jealous, since it accomplished nothing except to make him feel bad. He decided to let go of his resentment that Eric was successful, and instead become pro active and figure out how to be successful too. He put the focus back on himself and his business, talked with his mentors and other successful restaurateurs, and started making changes to bring in new customers.

Six months later Jay was a happier man. Not only because his business had picked up and his Deli was doing well, but because he no longer carried around the negativity that he had fostered with his jealousy.

Jealousy involves feeling threatened. In reality, feeling envious or jealous really means you're putting yourself down and valuing the other person's circumstances more than you value yourself. It's a sign you're feeling inadequate, incompetent, or uncomfortable with some aspect of yourself.

When you feel capable, competent, valuable and lovable on your own, there is no need to covet the abilities or possessions of others. It's only when your insecurities make themselves known that you think you need what others have.

If you notice the self-talk voice in your head saying things like: "I wish I looked like she does," "I hate them when they talk about all their money," or "I hope s/he drives that new car into a ditch," you're jealous and envious. Listen to your thoughts, to your words, and to your "gut," to determine if you're feeling insecure in some way.

There's a fine line between being envious and simply admiring another person. When you're able to accept who you are and feel compassion for yourself, you will be able to admire, appreciate, and be happy for others without wanting what they have for yourself. Feelings of envy and jealousy will fade.

Jealousy takes a tremendous amount of your energy. It blocks your ability to think and be productive, which interferes with feeling positive about yourself. Rather than focusing on others, think about what would happen if you channeled this energy into positive thoughts about yourself. It's so much more empowering, fun, and productive.

It's helpful to look at yourself in the mirror and appreciate the special person you are. Know that you're smart, kind, strong, resilient, capable, lovable, and valuable. It's these and many more internal qualities that make you the unique person you are, and that make it possible for you to eliminate feelings of envy and jealousy from your life.

You might find it useful to identify situations in which you have felt or currently feel envious or jealous of another person's circumstances or possessions. Identify your insecurities that foster these feelings, and then write down ways you can take care of yourself and eliminate these emotions from your life.

Guilt

Guilt is a complex emotion. At times, guilt can be positive because it lets you know you've violated one of your values. If you occasionally feel guilty, you probably have a strong sense of values and are a compassionate, caring individual who is aware of what's important to you and the effect your words and actions have on others.

When experienced at appropriate times, guilt lets you know you've done or thought something that feels uncomfortable for you because it in some way goes against your values and/or beliefs. Guilt reminds you to pay attention, examine your thoughts or behavior, and note which value has been compromised.

The important thing to remember is that guilt is like a red flag that pops up to alert you that something you're doing doesn't feel right. Once it's done its job, **it's not supposed to hang around** and make you feel awful. Once you acknowledge the red guilt flag and identify it's significance, you then need to **put it down**.

The problem arises when you allow that flag to stay up and keep waving strongly, which makes you continue to feel guilty. Once you notice the flag, your job is to examine and possibly rectify whatever caused it to pop up, and then let it go.

Guilt comes from two places: from yourself and your self-talk, or from others who try to lay guilt on you.

At times you might lay guilt on yourself, based on the self-talk and old or current messages in your head. You might even use guilt to 'punish' yourself for doing, saying, or thinking something that your values or beliefs tell you is 'wrong.'

When this happens you have the power to look at whatever you feel guilty about and decide whether you have truly violated your values. If you've disregarded a value you still believe in, then take action to rectify the situation and put down the guilt flag.

It's important to note that some of the values you learned when you were young might no longer be appropriate for you now. For example, you may have come from a family in which male/female roles were very specific. Our culture used to support the idea that it was a man's job to earn the money and a woman's job to raise the children and maintain the home. So if you're a woman who earns more money than your husband, or a man who would rather stay home and raise the children than be the breadwinner, you might feel guilty for this decision.

Remember, the values you were taught when you were a child fit the beliefs of your parents and the culture of their time. They might not be appropriate for the current culture or who you are as an adult today.

The good news is that as an independent adult you have the right to examine what you're feeling, re-evaluate and rewrite your beliefs and values, make behavioral changes, and adjust your actions accordingly.

Guilt is often used by one person to exert power and control over another. If someone wants to manipulate and control you, they might try to 'make you feel guilty' by tapping into your values and letting you know they're disappointed in you for failing. If you choose to accept these 'guilt trips' they can erode your sense of personal power and self-esteem.

Always remember that just because someone 'lays down guilt,' does NOT mean you have to pick it up and put it on. If you determine the guilt tripper is doing it for his/her own benefit, and that you did not violate your values, you can choose to put down the flag and ignore the guilt.

It's up to you to decide whether guilt is appropriate for you to feel in each situation. You can choose whether you want to accept it or not.

You might find it helpful to look at situations in which you feel, or have felt guilty. Look at the 'shoulds' you've violated, and decide whether they still apply in your life. If they do and you want to live that value, then you can change the behavior that made you feel guilty.

If you realize you violated someone else's 'should', one you choose not to live by, you can create or continue to live by your own value and belief. Either way, once you understand where the guilt came from and if it's appropriate for you, make sure to put down the guilt flag.

SHEILA'S STORY

Sheila was raised to always be nice, kind and gentle with people, and if she wasn't she was taught that she was a 'bad person'. This would result in her feeling guilty and horrible about herself. To avoid feeling this way she often wasn't completely honest, and was inclined to give in to people's demands when she didn't want to.

When she did honor herself and go against someone's wishes, they were sad or angry and she'd end up feeling guilty.

This was especially true when it came to dating. Since she wanted to avoid being a 'bad person' and feeling guilty, she always tried to say yes when a man asked her out, even if she didn't think he was the right kind of person for her.

Eventually the man would think they were in a relationship, even though Sheila was trying to figure out how to break up with him. When she finally became clear and told him they could no longer date, he would invariably be hurt, and then she would feel guilty.

After years of trying to make people happy and feeling increasingly bad about herself, Sheila decided to look at the reality of her belief that she should always take care of others or feel guilty about it.

She realized that the guilt she felt was because she was breaking a value she'd been taught long ago, and in fact that value didn't always fit into her adult life. At times the kindest thing to do was to be tactfully honest from the start, and also to honor herself and her needs as much as those of others.

Once she learned the lesson the guilt taught her she was able to modify her former value and belief, start taking care of herself as well as others, and let go of the guilt.

Shame

Shame is an emotional response to believing you're defective, damaged or unacceptable. Unlike guilt, which you feel when you've committed some action or behavior that violates one of your values, shame is the rejection of your whole self and all of who you are.

Hopefully you don't have shame in your world. If you do, it's important to understand that it comes from very negative self-talk (probably learned when you were a small child), that tells you that you are defective, unlovable, and will never be good enough.

If you were taught to be ashamed of yourself, it's time to learn that there is nothing wrong with you. You are a terrific human being and it's OK to be who you are.

Understand that the negative messages from your childhood, the ones that told you that you have no value, may have been incorporated into negative self-talk, which holds you down and reinforces your inability to see the value you bring to the world.

As you look at and sort out these messages, you will begin to see that they are not, and have never been, true. They came from people who were unhappy in their own lives, and took their misery out on you. Children are always beautiful, valuable and loveable, and if your significant adults couldn't see your value because of their own issues, it wasn't your fault.

Now it's time for you to re-examine these messages and see how flawed and untrue they are. Then replace them with positive self-talk that reinforces the beautiful person you are.

Forgiveness

Forgiveness is defined as letting go of resentment, blame, or anger caused by a perceived offense. This means pardoning the offender, releasing the grudge and wiping the slate clean. You can forgive those you feel have wronged you, and you can also forgive yourself if you feel that you've done something that violates your values or has been hurtful to you or someone else.

It is physically and emotionally exhausting to hold grudges against others, and/or beat yourself up with guilt and blame. Often a lack of forgiveness can make you physically ill. When you forgive yourself or another, you free yourself from carrying around the negativity and heavy energy that blame, resentment, and anger weigh on you.

When you forgive you also reclaim your power from a situation that caused you to feel guilty or violated. Regaining your power rather than feeling victimized will help you feel strong, capable, and competent.

When you choose to forgive, you're acknowledging that it's impossible to re-do the past. You're saying you're ready to look forward and move ahead, rather than look backward and hold on to things over which you have no control. The best you can do is learn whatever lessons you needed to get from the situation, and then let go of the anger, pain and resentment and look ahead to the positive future.

In order to forgive yourself or others, the first step is to release all resentment, bitterness, and blame. These are all victim emotions, which come from feeling powerless. When you feel powerless or inadequate you release responsibility for what happens in your life. When you accept no responsibility you allow others to make decisions for you or abuse you in some way. Then the natural thing to do is to blame the people you have given your power to.

When you were a child you didn't have the power to take care of yourself, so you were at the mercy of others. However, as an adult you can let go of old hurts because now you do have personal power and can choose to let go of blame and move ahead.

Forgiveness comes when you accept responsibility for your part in any situation, and take back your personal power.

It's important to remember that blaming keeps you in a powerless position. Through forgiving yourself or others you regain personal power and increase your self-esteem.

ELLIE'S STORY

When Ellie was in grade school her parents divorced and her father moved to another state. He'd always been emotionally distant, but she hoped that now she'd be able to interact with him without her mother and siblings there as a distraction, and they would be able to have a loving relationship.

Unfortunately, her father soon remarried and adopted his wife's two daughters, which made him even more distant from Ellie. Even though he was an adult and she was still a child, he expected her to reach out and create a relationship with him. When she didn't, he made her feel guilty and like she was the one failing in the relationship.

For many years Ellie craved a relationship with her father, and was confused and conflicted by her love for this absent man and her resentment and pain at being abandoned.

After years of harboring anger towards her father Ellie realized she was deciding to stay mad, and that this decision was taking a physical and emotional toll on her. She wrote in her journal about her feelings, and realized she was allowing her negativity towards him to define their relationship, because she was still reacting to him as her 10-year old self, not the 35-year old she'd become.

Once Ellie understood that her father is who he is, his behavior wasn't personal, and she was wasting her time and energy being angry, she was able to forgive him for what she felt were years of abandonment and emotional neglect. Forgiving him allowed her to take back her power as it pertained to her happiness with the relationship. She is still saddened that they can't have a closer relationship, but has forgiven him and let go of the self-destructiveness of her hurt, resentment and anger.

You might find it helpful to look at your life and identify whom you need to forgive. It may be someone else, or it might be you. Either way, to move from blame to forgiveness, ask yourself some questions:

- Who do I resent/blame and why?

- How does holding on to this resentment/blame serve me?

- What was my responsibility in this situation?

- What is the lesson for me in this?

- What will happen if I let it go?

- What are some ways I can let it go and forgive?

Remember that forgiveness comes when you let go of resentment and blame and accept responsibility for moving on.

Also, know that just because you forgive does not mean that you forget. There are lessons to be learned from every situation. Always make sure you learn and remember them, so you won't find yourself in the same situation again.

"The truth is that stress doesn't come from your boss, your kids, your spouse, traffic jams, health challenges, or other circumstances. It comes from your thoughts about these circumstances."

—Andrew Bernstein

"A lot of people resist transition and therefore never allow themselves to enjoy who they are. Embrace the change, no matter what it is; once you do, you can learn about the new world you're in and take advantage of it."

—Nikki Giovanni

"When we are no longer able to change a situation—we are challenged to change ourselves."

—Viktor E. Frankl

Chapter Eight: Stress, Transitions, Grief & Loss

"If you are distressed by anything external, the pain is not due to the thing itself but to your own estimate of it; and this you have the power to revoke at any moment." —*Marcus Aurelius*

Stress

Stress is an inescapable part of life. Although it's often looked upon as negative, it can also be positive. When experienced intermittently, stress can be a motivating force that helps you accomplish a goal or meet a deadline. However, when experienced continually over a long period of time, it can become deadly!

What's important is for you to be aware of your mental and physical reactions to stress. When your body is under stress it experiences physiological changes that prepare it for "flight or fight," even though these days the actual need to fight or flee is not often necessary. Nevertheless, the body still prepares itself by tensing muscles, releasing adrenaline, and sharpening senses. For a short duration, this bodily response can be used positively to deal with whatever the stressor may be. However, if prolonged, as is often the case where daily life is filled with a wide variety of loud noises, stagnant air, traffic, hectic schedules, and demands and deadlines, the body system can be fatigued to the point of malfunctioning.

When this happens, you could experience physical symptoms

such as tightening of the jaw, stomachaches, clenched fists, tense shoulders, headaches, backaches, insomnia, sore muscles, mental confusion, eczema, weakened immune system, and a wide variety of other stress-related illness. It's also important to know that stress can temporarily cloud your perceptions and diminish self-confidence.

"Burnout" is a relatively new term used to describe what happens to a person experiencing long-term stress. For example, if you are an executive who continually deals with angry employees, demanding customers, and government regulations, you may eventually become so stressed that your body and mind "shut down." Then the physiological symptoms of stress may take over. Burnout occurs when you ignore the warning signs along the way, and do nothing to relieve the mental, emotional, and physical strains on your body.

There are many ways you can deal with the stress of daily life. Relaxation exercises, positive self-talk, meditation or quieting the mind, physical exercise, yoga, listening to calming music and being out in nature can all effectively calm the stress reaction and relieve the tension in your mind and body.

You might find it helpful to look at the things in your life that cause you stress, and note the physical and mental reactions you have to them. Then look at alternative, healthier ways to deal with these things. If you can identify and alleviate some of your life stress, you'll find your days run smoother and your physical, emotional, and mental condition will be much improved.

Christine's Story

Christine remembers being very stressed and thinking that if she didn't make some life changes she would probably get sick.

The stress Christine felt was a direct result of decisions she was making that dishonored herself and the people she purported to love. She was confused about several situations in her life, and was staying stuck because she was afraid to move in any direction that would change things. In the process she was being dishonest with herself, which was causing her huge stress.

Eventually she was diagnosed with a serious autoimmune disorder, and her doctors told her the potentially life-threatening disease had no known cause. However Christine knew without a doubt that all the poor choices she'd made—and didn't want to address— had weakened her immune system and manifested in a physical impairment.

Since her avoidance was literally making her sick she'd have no choice—if she wanted to live a long, healthy life —but to take a hard look at the way she was living and make different choices as she moved forward.

Making those changes required introspection. Christine began to understand that long ago when she was being pressured to make choices that were uncomfortable for her, she should have stopped trying to please everyone, relieved her stress and chosen to put herself first.

Today, Christine's autoimmune condition is under control. She's still being treated but the condition rarely affects her quality of life except when it acts as a barometer. If Christine is living in accordance with her values, her stress is low and her health is stable. When she goes off track and her health worsens, Christine appreciates the reminder to stop, take stock, make better decisions and reduce her stress.

Transition, Grief, and Loss

"Change is the law of life, and those who look only to the past or present are certain to miss the future." —*John F. Kennedy*

Change, transition, and the loss that goes with them are a normal and frequent part of life. Transition can be defined as anything that temporarily or permanently disrupts your normal routine and creates change in your life. It can be anything from a child starting school in the fall, a job promotion, moving to a new home, the birth of a baby, loss of a friend, or even death. The perception you have of a transition or loss is often related to uncertainty about how you feel about yourself and your ability to deal with it.

Transitions can be both positive and negative. They can include things you celebrate such as the achievement of a long-term goal like graduation or marriage, to the loss of a special person or place in your life. They may be the result of your choices, or may be unwanted occurrences over which you have no control. Some changes might represent the final closing of a chapter in your life, while others may be more temporary.

Whatever the transition, it will require you to let go of an old established pattern of thinking and acting, and learn ways to deal with whatever the new situation is. Transitioning requires flexibility, emotional growth, and willingness to change on your part

An important aspect of the change process involves grieving for what was. Grieving usually occurs even if the loss or change is for the better.

The process of adapting to change and grieving for what has been lost usually brings up several different emotions, which you will experience to varying degrees, depending on the impact the change has made in your life.

In order to work through this process you might find it helpful to understand the stages of grief and look at the steps involved in moving through them.

DENIAL. Often the first part of this emotional process is shock or denial. During this time you tell yourself that whatever has happened is "no big deal." Self-talk phrases such as "I can handle this," "Let's just get on with it," are common during this period, and your feelings are fairly numb. Even though your feelings are numb, your body may still be reacting. You could have sweaty palms, tense muscles, headaches, stomachaches, digestive problems, difficulty thinking or focusing and a variety of other physical symptoms.

ANGER/DEPRESSION. Eventually the reality of the transition will dawn on you, and at this point you may become either angry or depressed, or alternate between the two. The anger can be frightening because it's often irrational and unpredictable. It may be directed at people who are not even involved in your situation, or at God, your Higher Power, or even yourself. It often appears when you least expect it, and it can feel overpowering.

Depression is also frightening because during this time emotions are overwhelming and you can find yourself crying "for no reason," have difficulty concentrating, experience memory loss, be unable to carry on conversations or even motivate yourself to get out of bed. During this time your body also experiences a great sense of fatigue and you might feel physically exhausted most of the time

In this stage, sitting and staring at the wall may be all you can manage, and THIS IS OK! Although this experience can be frightening for a normally active, intelligent person, the best thing you can do for yourself during this time is to do whatever feels right, as long as it's not harmful to others or yourself. If that means mentally shutting down for a while and allowing your emotions time to heal, then that's what is most therapeutic for you and what you should allow yourself to do.

GUILT. Another feeling that can be associated with grief is guilt. If you are dealing with a negative transition there may be a sense of self-blame, or over-responsibility. You might mentally relive the experience or situation and spend a lot of time trying to redo it in your mind. This is also part of the bargaining phase, where you may mentally try to make a deal with your Higher Power to change or alter the situation. For example, a parent who has a seriously ill child might vow to live a better life or help others more if the child recovers.

ACCEPTANCE. Eventually you will reach a state of acceptance, where you have managed to let go of the old, fit the new into your life, and come to terms with the change. The old way of living has become a permanent part of the whole incredible you, and has contributed to the new person you are continuously becoming.

The grief process takes no predictable amount of time. It's a very personal and individual experience, and how you go through it depends on the transition and the depth of influence on your life. However, it usually takes longer than people expect, and it's most important to trust your feelings during this time.

It's also important to recognize that there are some huge losses you might never 'get over'. However, time helps, and you will eventually be able to focus on the positive and move ahead with your life.

If someone has left or died and you find you can't move ahead from grieving after a year or two, you need to check and see if you're holding on to your grief as a way of staying connected to or honoring the person who has left. Some people are afraid if they allow themselves to move past the grief they are disrespecting the person who is no longer with them. If a loved one has died, it's important to remember that life is for the living, and that the person who is gone wouldn't want you to waste yours looking back. Most likely they would want you to look ahead and live the best life you can in their honor.

When you are grieving, you might find it helpful to have a trusted confidant to talk with about your memories, regrets, fears, joys and feelings. Talking helps you process what you're feeling and come to terms with how things will change.

Writing and keeping a Feeling Journal can also be powerful on your road to moving past your grief and healing.

JOE'S STORY

When Joe's marriage ended he found himself going through the grief process. He was overwhelmed, confused and at times felt out of control. He compared his grieving to standing on an ocean beach with his toes at the water line. His feelings of grief were like the water.

He noticed that at times the waves would come in and the water was around his knees, making him aware of its cold presence but not causing too much distress. At other times the water would tickle his toes, so he was conscious of it, but it didn't impact him much. Occasionally the water came in more forcefully and slammed him in his chest, almost knocking him off his feet and taking his breath away. Then, once in a while a giant wave would come, overwhelm him, knock him to the sand and try to suck him away. When this happened all he could do was breathe and hang on by his fingernails.

Joe realized that grief is as unpredictable and powerful as the ocean, and the way to get through it is the same as dealing with the sea. He understood he couldn't control it, but he could hang on, ride it out, and eventually the storm would pass and he could move ahead and be OK.

Transitional experiences and the resulting grief foster personal growth. They consist of life's triumphs and tragedies, and are a necessary part of a complete, full life. Although understanding the process won't alleviate the pain, knowing how it works and what to expect may take the fear and confusion out of it for you.

Significant, transitional life events are opportunities for your personal path of growth. It's important for you to know that the event is not what's important. What matters is the process and how you deal with it. What you learn from each event makes you stronger, and adds to your ability to take on and deal effectively with whatever the next situation will be.

As you experience transition, change and loss throughout your life, you gain an appreciation for your flexibility, strength, and ability to cope and adapt. Your self-esteem and image of yourself as a capable, competent person will continue to grow as you deal with difficult life situations. The more difficult and painful the transition or event, the greater your personal growth can be.

You might find it helpful to take a few minutes to think of some transitions you have walked through, and remember how you felt during the experience. Draw a line that represents your life (straight, curved, whatever feels right).

Think for a minute about the positive and negative significant events you've experienced. Write these events on your lifeline, marking them with an "X" and identifying the event and any people who were an important part of it. Begin with your earliest memory of childhood and continue to the present.

Then identify how it felt for you, what was gained or lost, and your fears about it. Think about how you dealt with these feelings, what you learned about yourself in the process, and the ways the experience changed you.

Stages of the Grief Process

The chart on the following page describes the stages of the grief process, and the thoughts, feelings, and physical changes you can expect as you walk through it.

STAGES	DENIAL/SHOCK	ANGER	GUILT	BARGAINING	DEPRESSION	ACCEPTANCE
DESCRIBE	Don't want to believe or accept. This is really no big deal.	Lashing out, mad or upset. Rage for no reason. Irrational.	Feel responsible. Self-blaming.	Make a deal with God or whomever. Try to change or redo situation. Contract. If I ___ then you ___.	Down, sad, alone, left-out, withdrawn.	Letting go. Ability to go forward with life. Renewed energy & self-esteem.
WORDS & THOUGHTS	It's not true. I know it will turn out to be a mistake. This is just a dream.	I HATE YOU! This is unfair. It's all your fault. I'll get you for this.	What did I do? It's all MY fault. I always do it wrong. They'd be better off without me.	I'll promise to do/ be ___ if only this isn't true. Try to redo/ undo situation.	I don't care. It's HOPELESS. It will never be OK again. What's the point of trying?	It's OK. I can handle it. Things will be all right now. I still have a life and can go on.
FEELINGS/ ACTIONS	Act like nothing has happened. Avoid issue. Feel numb and stunned. More/ less active.	Frustration, irritability, pouting, sulking, raging. Verbal & physical hostility. Attacking.	Blame self. Take responsibility for situations you did not cause.	Do better at activities. Act overly mature or responsible.	Hopelessness. Helplessness. Uncontrollable crying, moodiness, fear of being rejected. Loss of weight. Insomnia.	Increased trust in self & others. New sense of purpose. Sense of future. Relief. New self-esteem and confidence.
BODILY SIGNS & SYMPTOMS	Muted affect. Hyperactivity. Physical exhaustion. Insomnia. Restless or sleeps a lot.	Increased heart rate. Shortness of breath. Insomnia. Headaches. Chest pains. Mood swings.	Headaches. Chest pain. Muscular tension. Fatigue. Upset stomach. Diarrhea.	Increased heart rate. Insomnia. Muscular tension. Diarrhea. Anxiety. Headaches. Chest pain.	Mental and emotional confusion. Disorientation. Loss of appetite or overeating. Can't concentrate. Tired all time. Weight loss/gain. Overly emotional.	Return to normal in all bodily functions.

There are several things you can do for yourself if you are dealing with grief:

1. RECOGNIZE ALL OF THE LOSSES.

In most loss situations you will have lost more than just one thing. When there is a death of a loved one, you not only lose the presence of the deceased, but also the future you were planning, the security of having that person there, the everyday interaction, and your identity as spouse, parent, friend, etc., the dream of "happily ever after."

In the not-so-obvious-loss situation you might not even realize you are grieving. For example, the selling of the family car can spur feelings of grief. In this situation you are not only losing a known quantity, but are also letting go of something that has been an integral part of your family. This vehicle probably played a part in many memories, both positive and negative, that form the history of your family. It provided transportation when you brought your first child home from the hospital, when you got your puppy, that wonderful trip to the coast, etc. No matter how insignificant it seems, it has become part of who you are, and its loss will make some kind of impact.

2. BE WITH THE FEELINGS

It's OK to feel anger, frustration, guilt, anxiety, pain, depression and anything else that may come up. IT IS NORMAL, and is a sign that you're able to respond to life's experiences. Although shock/denial is part of the process, try not to deny or cover over your feelings for a long period of time --- this hinders the healing process. Be with the feelings, whatever they are, so the healing process can begin.

3. SUPPORT

Since loss is part of living, everyone experiences it at some time. The task is to help yourself move through it, from immediate loss to eventual gain, as rapidly, smoothly, and comfortably as possible. You can help yourself by finding people to support you. Being willing to talk about the change and your feelings relating to it will help you move through the process. Don't be afraid to mention your loss and open the conversation so they can talk with you about it. If you are grieving, find a person or a support group, who can fill this vital role for you.

4. LOSING IS NOT FAILING

Regardless of your loss, your self-confidence might suffer a jolt. Often thoughts are filled with guilt, worry, inadequacy, anger and self-hatred. These thoughts are all symptoms of the grief process. Some people tend to punish themselves with "if only" statements (if only I had/hadn't done this or that, this thing wouldn't have happened and I wouldn't have to deal with it or be in this emotional state now). This is normal, although counter productive, and is part of the Bargaining phase of the process.

5. RESOLUTION

Yes, there is an end to each loss situation. If it is a major transition or huge loss, you may never forget. However, if you allow yourself to, you will eventually come to a place of acceptance and be able to get on with your life. Life may never be 'the same', but you will be able to move ahead and make it as positive as it can be.

If the loss is smaller, the entire process may take a very short time. Everyone does it in his/her own time and own way. It's important to remember there is no right way to grieve. Whatever the feelings are, and however long it takes, is right for you. Just remember time does heal and there will be an end to the suffering.

6. IT TAKES TIME

Even though we know intellectually that there will be an

end to the intense feelings, there might be a tendency to rush the process to get past the pain, anxiety, inconsistencies and mental confusion. Always remember that HEALING TAKES TIME! It's important to allow yourself to do it in the time and way that works for you.

7. THE ROLLER COASTER EFFECT

The process of moving through the stages of grief is a bumpy one. It's like riding a roller coaster—up and down, fast and slow, around and around. You won't move neatly through each stage. It's common to bounce around and experience several stages in a short time. When you are grieving the people around you need to know there will be inconsistencies in your emotions and behavior. You may find that you have little or no control over whatever you're feeling. These changes take place in a matter of minutes, hours or days. Just know that you will eventually get off the roller coaster and return to a smoother, straighter, calmer ride.

If you are grieving, some things you can do to help yourself are:

- Pay attention to your emotions and allow yourself to feel them.

- Talk it out with someone you trust

- Find a peaceful spot and be quiet for awhile

- Exercise or do hobbies that will work you physically and mentally

- Do something for others

- Take things slowly and be patient and gentle with yourself

- Find the humor and laugh when you can

Remember that even if the pain returns from time to time throughout your life, you can recover and resume living in a new way.

Chapter Nine: Who Am I?

Why I Like ME!

Even if you're not in touch with your many special characteristics, it's important for you to know that you have them and that they are what make you unique.

They may be qualities that you discount as 'no big deal,' or think everyone has. Or, you might have been taught when you were young to only focus on the negative, be modest, and avoid bragging. As a result, you eventually learned to discount the beautiful, wonderful person you are. It's a shame to compare yourself negatively with others, and not allow yourself to be honest about the things that make you special.

It's time for you to acknowledge and be proud of who you are. It's time to get past all the '*shoulds*' that tell you you're an unlovable, valueless, ordinary person, and to get in touch with the special, capable, competent, loveable, unique being that is the true you.

If you can't think of anything special about you, ask yourself some questions:

- **Am I a good friend?** What qualities do I have that make me the kind of person people want for a friend? Am I loyal, fun, thoughtful, kind, supportive, a good listener, and trustworthy, etc.?

- **Am I a good employee?** Then I must be punctual, honest, smart, capable, reliable, responsible, and a good communicator, etc.

- **Am I a good partner or parent?** Then I must be loving, protective, caring, consistent, gentle, firm, thoughtful, and reliable, etc.

- **Am I a good athlete or great at my hobbies?** Then I must be athletic, coordinated, strong, motivated, creative, artistic, talented, clever, courageous, and daring.

Try to come up with a list of at least ten (or more) qualities that you like about yourself. No modesty allowed here! It's important to be honest with yourself about what makes you special. Be sure to include all of your qualities, even if you think they're not totally unique.

It's time to accept that there are MANY characteristics you are secretly proud of, and let the words flow. This list is only for you, and can serve as positive affirmations about yourself when you preface each characteristic with the words, "I am."

Hang it on your bathroom mirror or someplace handy, and read it several times a day. Trust that this list represents your intuition about the person you really are, and start believing it with your conscious mind.

JEFF'S STORY

Jeff was a shy child and was turning into a shy adult when he fell into a position that put him in the spotlight. Because of his presence and intelligence he was offered a position on live television. He was surprised to discover he was comfortable on-camera, but he hated when viewers felt the need to take out their dissatisfaction with the news by being critical of him. On more than one occasion Jeff took phone calls from viewers unhappy about everything from the way he dressed to the way he looked and sounded.

Many comments were hurtful, and about parts of Jeff that he couldn't control like his facial features and voice. Jeff liked and was good at his job, but frequently didn't want to answer the phone or read e-mail for fear of being attacked. He also became self-conscious about his appearance, wondering how to become "masculine enough" to stop the disparaging remarks.

Over time, Jeff's skin thickened and the comments stopped hurting so much. He took joy in doing his job well and found that the more he developed his skills and took pride in his work, the less the negativity bothered him. With the help of his seasoned colleagues he learned that he would never be able to make everyone happy, and that as long as he liked himself, there would always be at least one person in the room happy with him.

Now, Jeff has a positive relationship with himself and knows that his happiness will attract like-minded people. He lets negativity fall by the wayside and feels empathy for those who have the need to lash out at others. He no longer internalizes negative comments or feels the need to please everyone or defend his choices. He is becoming adept at standing up for himself without becoming emotional or giving away his power.

Jeff has learned he likes himself and can be his own best friend in the same way he would be a friend to another person—by listening to and respecting his needs, and being gentle and supportive with himself. He now knows his relationship with himself affects every other part of his life and so nurtures it as he does all his other relationships.

Humor and Laughter

"The shortest line between two people is humor." —*Victor Borge*

Humor and laughter are essential ingredients in creating a perfect day and a healthy, happy life. Humor is the playful, whimsical, joyful way you observe life. Laughter is your response to what you find humorous, and often it mirrors who you are.

It's been proven that finding the fun and joy, and laughing at life's silliness and absurdities is healthy behavior. Amazingly, appreciating the funny side of life can actually improve your emotional and physical condition. When you laugh, your body relaxes, secretes endorphins in your brain, and assists your immune system in keeping you healthy. Laughter also provides a sense of well-being, contentment, joy, and boosts your spirit and the attitude of those around you.

Laughter is one of the key ingredients in coping with daily stress. It can often diffuse tension and anger, and turn enemies into friends. If you look for the humor in a situation you will probably find it.

No two people respond exactly the same to humor. Some may not react at all to what you think is funny, while others may belly laugh with you.

You might think having a sense of humor means having the ability to tell jokes. However, it has little to do with joke telling. Humor comes in many forms, and is really a very personal part of who you are. Regardless of the source or form of humor, what's important is that it's positive and enhancing to all concerned. Make sure your humor is gentle. Your ability to do this indicates that you have compassion for yourself and others.

Negative humor at another person's expense is cruel, destructive and can cause pain and hurt feelings. Cruelty is never funny!

Your ability to appreciate humor and find the fun allows you to be happy as you walk through life. It also helps others want to enjoy the process along with you.

Always be sure to appreciate yourself and your ability to find the fun and joy in life. It makes all the difference.

Remember: "You don't stop laughing when you grow old. You grow old when you stop laughing." —George Bernard Shaw

Good Decisions

"Good judgment comes from experience, which comes from bad judgment." —*Will Rogers*

Every day you're confronted with opportunities to make decisions. They can be big or small, anything from where to go for lunch, to whether to buy that new car, get married, have a child, or change your career. Whatever your choice, there is usually an outcome you'd like to achieve. Sometimes you're successful and sometimes you're not.

Regardless of the end result, you probably learn something from the decision-making process you use to settle on a course of action. Learn from the experience, so you will be able to repeat your success or avoid making similar errors in the future. Remember that all decisions provide you with an opportunity to learn.

Decisions can be made on an intellectual, intuitive, or emotional basis. Pay attention to the way you make decisions and what process feels most comfortable for you.

You also need to know that with any decision, you most likely do the best you can at the time with *the information and resources available*. It's a waste of time to use hindsight and new information that comes later, to chastise yourself for a decision whose outcome was not what you desired. If the outcome was not what you wanted, *be gentle with yourself and learn the lesson* so the next outcome will be more positive.

Making decisions that work for you helps you feel good about yourself and increases your self-confidence and can build your self-esteem. It reminds you what an intelligent, capable, competent person you are. Making unwise decisions can also reinforce your sense of self-worth if you choose to learn and grow from them.

You might find it helpful to take a few minutes to reflect on your life, and think of several important decisions you've made. Look at the mechanism you used to arrive at these decisions (intellect, intuition, or emotion) and decide if that process eventually resulted in a wise or unwise choice. Also, note what you learned about yourself through the process, and determine whether you'd do the same thing again, or how you'd do it differently next time.

JERRY'S STORY

Jerry was always told he was stupid and would never be able to accomplish much in his life. When he was young he believe this, and choose to just let life slide by with minimum effort.

When he was in third grade he had a Scout leader who saw a hidden spark in Jerry, and focused on empowering him so he would start to believe in himself. The leader gave Jerry responsibilities within the troop and supported him as he tackled them.

Jerry began to see that he was capable and smart, and that his family's early predictions of his potential might not be accurate. He decided to work hard, despite their negativity, to set and accomplish goals. As Jerry moved ahead and had more and more successes, he decided on the career he wanted and how he would get the education to reach it.

By the time Jerry graduated from high school with a full scholarship to the college of his choice, he was able to look back and pinpoint the time when he started making wise decisions for himself. He realized that all the decisions he'd made, and what he'd learned from each of them, were important to his eventual success.

Favorite Things

What do you like? What's fun for you? What is your favorite season, smell, place and taste? You are unique, and part of how you express that uniqueness is in your preferences. What you like and dislike, and favorite things that you might not have given much thought to, are all keys to the amazing individual that is you!

What you see, hear, smell, touch, and do all create perceptions and feelings for you, so your personal preferences are an important indication of who you are. Because of this, it's important for you to be aware of these things and bring them into your consciousness and your life whenever possible.

Your favorite things are a reflection of who you are today, and also who you used to be. They are a combination of memories, former likes, and current preferences, and all add up to an important aspect of the unique person you are.

You might find it fun to spend some time noticing what's important to you, and acknowledging what brings you joy. Do you have a favorite season or one you really dislike? Does the sun on your face, the smell of flowers in the spring, or the hug of a special person make you happy? Sometimes it's amazing to compile a list and see how many things bring you joy.

Take a few minutes to get in touch with yourself and have fun thinking about your favorite things. Always remember that your personal preferences are an important part of what makes you unique.

If you make a point of being aware of these things as you go through each day, you'll discover that you bring them into your life more often and that you'll find yourself smiling and enjoying your days and yourself more than you ever have.

My Values, Attitudes, and Core Beliefs

At the beginning of this book you spent time examining, in a loving, nonjudgmental manner, the basic belief systems of your parents or significant adults, and the family and culture you were raised in. Now it's time for you to do the same with your own beliefs and values.

Spend some time looking at the way you choose to run your life. Are your attitudes and behavior 'rules' identical to the ones you were raised with, or have you modified them to meet the needs of the person you are now?

Notice that many of your values are probably the same as those you were raised with, and in most instances that's a good thing. Values such as paying your bills on time, being responsible and reliable, treating others as you would like to be treated, obeying the laws of the land, and treating your body and yourself with respect are good values that guide you in being a healthy and reliable person, friend, family member, and citizen.

However, there might be other values you were taught as a child, that you are still living by, that no longer serve you well. Some of these could be about your worth and rights as a person, outdated role beliefs such as "It's the man's job to earn the money and the woman's job to take care of the house," or "Others are always right so keep quiet and let them run things."

Be clear about the values, attitudes, and beliefs you're currently choosing to live your life by. Note whether they really serve you well, or if they are just ideas you were taught long ago that you've always followed.

Please remember that **as an adult you always have the right to change** whatever no longer fits the person you are now. Any time you want, you can create new rules that will work for you and the person you are today.

You might find it helpful to take time to think about and write down your current attitudes, beliefs, 'shoulds' and feelings, and then go back to those you thought about in Chapter Two. Are they the same, similar but different in some areas, or totally opposite?

Then look at how these beliefs, values and 'shoulds' impact your life today.

The purpose of doing this is to help you become aware of the ways you're currently choosing to run your life. To see if it's truly YOUR life, or merely a carbon copy of what once worked for your parents, family, and culture.

While you're doing this, remember that those who gave you these values taught you the best they could at the time. However, they had no way of knowing who you would be as an adult, or what values would work for you throughout your life. The awareness of what is truly important to YOU will help build and strengthen your personal power and self-esteem.

If you identify old beliefs and patterns that no longer serve you well or fit into today's culture, you have the right to change them.

Remember that:

- Your parents and significant adults helped shape your values, attitudes, and beliefs.

- Your current values are probably different in some ways than those of your parents, which is fine.

- YOU choose how you want to run your life; no one else knows what's right for you as an adult.

- It's your right to give yourself permission to change your values when they no longer work for you.

- You don't need anyone else's permission to choose and live by your own values.

JUDI'S STORY

Judi, like most of us, was raised to believe many things were good or right, and many were bad or wrong. These were the values and beliefs of her parents, family, friends, and culture, which were passed along to her and guided her as she grew.

For the most part she agreed with what she'd been

taught, but there were several things that fit her parent's lifestyle but didn't fit hers once she was an adult.

Because of this she was always conflicted, trying to fit herself into the framework they'd made for her, but realizing that some of it didn't work for her. When she chose to live the way that did work for her but violated their values, she ended up feeling guilty about it.

Eventually Judi became tired of always feeling uncomfortable with herself because she was trying to live someone else's life. She decided to look at the beliefs that were causing her trouble (such as "good mothers stay home and raise their children instead of having a career") and gave herself permission to rewrite the values into ones that fit who she is rather than who her parents were.

Her new value system is a compilation of many things she learned as a child, and many more that she's learned as an adult. By allowing herself to let go of the ones that no longer fit who she is now, creating new values to take their place, and combining these with the old that still work for her, she's created her own set of values and beliefs by which to guide her life.

Your Epitaph

As you've read through this book you've looked at:

- The positive and negative values, attitudes, and beliefs you learned from your family, culture, and significant others.

- The importance of feeling compassion, love and appreciation for yourself rather than guilt, anger, frustration, or shame.

- Why your self-talk and feelings are so important.

- Who you were when you were younger, and who you are now.

• The many reasons you are a lovable, valuable person.

As you reflect on these things, think about how you would like to be remembered by those who've known you. What special qualities do you possess that you want to be associated with your memory? Are you kind, creative, loving, supportive, fun, efficient, generous, smart, etc.? Think about what you would like to have written in your obituary and also on your tombstone about the person you are and how you lived your life?

This process can take some thought, and will probably serve as a guide in your own journey of personal growth. It's one more way for you to get in touch with your deep inner goals. It will show you what's most important to you.

JOHN'S STORY

When John was writing his Epitaph he began with a long summation about how he loved his wife and children, and enjoyed his job, friends and activities. When it was explained to him that the Epitaph was to go on his tombstone, John, who spoke no Spanish, summarized it with, "I've had a great life! Adios!"

The Big Question

Imagine you are dying. What is the one question you will ask yourself about your life? What was it all about for you? For some people the question is "Did I love?" "Was I helpful?", "Was I kind?", "Did I succeed?", "Was I a terrific business person?", "Was I a great parent or friend?" or "Did I make a difference?" There is no right or wrong answer to this question. It's very personal, and reflects who you are and what's most important to you.

Look at how you're currently living your life, and decide if it will give you a positive answer to the Big Question, or if there are some things you might want to change while you still have time.

My Rediscovered Self

Throughout this book you've looked at many aspects of your personality and all the things that make you such a unique and incredible human being. These are aspects of yourself that you may have been in touch with when you were a child. However, through the growth process and the necessity to adapt to your environment, you might have lost contact with some of them. Hopefully, while reading this book you've been able to look at and reconnect with many of these lost parts.

This is a summary of what you have been rediscovering. Be sure to take time to go back over whatever points had special meaning for you, or ones that you wanted to avoid (that's a sign that it's an issue for you).

Also take some time to think about all you have learned, and then answer the following questions:

My major values are _____

My skills, talents and abilities are_____

My interests are _____

I lose track of time when I'm _____

My greatest strengths are _____

Several things I'm proud of myself for are _____

Things I want to let go of are _____

Things I'm proud of myself about are _____

Things I like about myself are _____

Times I have felt successful _____

My major needs are _____

My main life goals are _____

Always remember to tell yourself that:

"I AM AN INCREDIBLE, LOVEABLE, VALUABLE, UNIQUE PERSON!"

Chapter Ten:
Moving Forward

AS YOU'VE READ this book you've had the opportunity to look at who you are and how you became this amazing, unique individual. You've identified values, attitudes, beliefs, and behaviors you were taught as a child, and noted which still work for you today. Hopefully you've also given yourself permission to change the ones that no longer fit who you are now.

You've become aware of the importance of your rights and the value of claiming your personal power in relating to others.

You've looked at the connection between your thoughts and feelings, and understand that you are in charge of your self-talk. You now know that through your self-talk, you have the power to create your own positive or negative feelings and emotional responses, which will result in how you choose to feel and act. There is no room to blame others. Your feelings and resulting behavior are completely your responsibility. Only yours.

Parts of this journey might have been painful, but if you've gotten this far through this book I hope you're feeling proud and joyful! Self-discovery can be difficult, but also incredibly rewarding and life changing.

The fact that you've had the courage to look honestly at where you came from and who you are now, complete with skills, attitudes, beliefs, values, fears, insecurities, likable/unlikable characteristics, preferences and dreams, shows that you are strong, insightful, and courageous enough to grow, learn, and become the best you can be.

This might have been a difficult yet joyful journey of rediscovering the special person you've always been. Hopefully from now on you will accept yourself in totality, and feel love and compassion for your whole being.

Congratulations! You now have the power to be free, self aware, and all you can be! This is what self-esteem is all about.

References

Alberti, Robert E., and Emmons, M.L. *Your Perfect Right: A Guide to Assertive Behavior.* San Luis Obispo, California: Impact Publishers, Inc., 1970, 1974, 1978, 1982.

Barksdale, Lilburn S. *Building Self-Esteem.* 2nd Edition. Idyllwild, California: Barksdale Foundation, 1989.

Branden, Nathaniel. *How to Raise Your Self-Esteem.* New York: Bantam Books, 1988.

Brooks, B. David, and Dalby, Rex K. *The Self-Esteem Maintenance and Repair Manual.* Newport Beach, California: Kincaid House, 1989.

Buscaglia, Leo. *Love.* New York: Fawcett, 1981.

Clark, Jean. *Self-Esteem: A Family Affair.* New York: Harper and Row, 1980.

Davis, Laura, and Bass, Ellen. *The Courage to Heal Workbook: A Guide for Women Survivors of Child Sexual Abuse.* New York: Perennial Library, 1988.

Davis, M.; Eshelman, E.; and McKay, M. *The Relaxation and Stress Reduction Workbook. 2nd Edition.* Richmond, California: New Harbinger Publications, 1982.

Elkins, Dov P. *Teaching People to Love Themselves: Leader's Handbook of Theory and Techniques.* Beachwood, Ohio: Growth Associates, 1977.

Hagberg, Janet. *Real Power.* Minneapolis, Minnesota: Winston Press, 1984.

Helmstetter, Shad. *The Self-Talk Solution.* New York: Morrow Publishers, 1988.

Hendricks, Gay. *Learning to Love Yourself: A Guide to Becoming Centered.* New York: Prentice Hall Press, 1982.

Homey, Karen. *Neurosis and Human Growth: The Struggle Toward Self-Realization.* New York: Norton and Company, Inc., 1950.

Jung, Carl G., and others. *Man and His Symbols.* Garden City, New York: Doubleday, 1964.

Kehayan, V. Alex. *Self-Awareness Growth Experience that Promote Positive Self-Esteem.* Rolling Hills, California: Jalmar Press, Subsidiary of B.L. Winch and Associates, 1989.

Landorf, Joyce. *Balcony People.* Waco, Texas: Word Books, 1984.

McKay, M.; Davis, Martha; and Fanning, Patrick. *Thoughts and Feelings, The Art of Cognitive Stress Intervention.* Richmond, California: New Harbinger Publications, 1981.

Napoleon, J. & Abell, S. *Self-Esteem: An Inside Job.* Medford, Oregon. Inside Jobs Publishing Co. 1990.

Palladino, Connie. *Developing Self-Esteem.* Los Altos, California: Crisp Publications, 1989.

Palmer, Pat, Ed.D. *Liking Myself.* San Luis Obispo, California: Impact Publishers, Inc., 1977.

Porat, Frieda. *Self-Esteem: The Key to Success in Work and Love.* Billings, Montana: R&E Publications, 1988.

Sehnert, Keith. *Stress / Unstress.* Minneapolis, Minnesota: Augsburg Publishers, 1981.

Viorst, Judith. *Necessary Losses.* New York: Simon and Schuster, 1986.

Wilcox, Gloria. *Training Manual for Facilitators*, Inner Growth Seminar Handouts. Palo Alto, California, 1979.

Wegscheider-Cruse, Sharon. *Learning to Love Yourself: Finding Your Self-Worth.* Deerfield Beach, Florida: Health Communications, 1987.

Wells, Joel. *Who Do You Think You Are? How to Build Self-Esteem.* Chicago, Illinois: Thomas More Publishers, 1989.

ABOUT THE AUTHOR

Sandra Abell is a Business and Life Coach and Licensed Professional Counselor. She has been in private practice for more than 20 years, and is the president of Inside Jobs Coaching Company. She received her undergraduate degree from San Jose State University in California, her graduate degree from Southern Oregon State University in Ashland, Oregon, and is a graduate of Coach University in Colorado Springs, CO. She is a member of the International Coach Federation and the International Association of Coaches, and specializes in working with business owners, professionals, entrepreneurs and people in transition. She concentrates on helping people move ahead, accomplish goals and maximize their potential in every area of their lives. Sandy can be reached at www.insidejobscoach.com.

Books by Sandra Abell:

Feeling Good About You: The Journey of Discovery that Leads to Self-Esteem

Reflections On Life and Love

Books by Sandra Abell and Janice Napoleon:

Moving Up To Management: Leadership and Management Skills for New Supervisors

Moving Up To Management: Leadership and Management Skills for Caregivers

Self-Esteem: An Inside Job